The Best of
LONDON
Capital of Cool

David Hampshire

CITY BOOKS

City Books • Bath • England

First published 2017

City Books, c/o Survival Books Limited
Office 169, 3 Edgar Buildings
George Street, Bath BA1 2FJ, United Kingdom
+44 (0)1305-246283, info@survivalbooks.net
www.survivalbooks.net and www.londons-secrets.com

British Library Cataloguing in Publication Data
A CIP record for this book is available
from the British Library.
ISBN: 978-1-909282-92-6

Printed in China

Acknowledgements

The author would like to thank all the many people who helped with research and provided information for this book. Special thanks are due to Gwen Simmonds for her invaluable research, Graeme & Louise Chesters and Richard Todd; Robbi Atilgan for editing; Peter Read for additional editing and proof-reading; David Woodworth for final proof checking; John Marshall for DTP, photo selection and cover design; and the author's partner (Alexandra) for the constant supply of tea and coffee.

Last, but not least, a special thank you to the many photographers – the unsung heroes – whose beautiful images bring London to life.

IMPORTANT

Before visiting anywhere without unrestricted access it's advisable to check the opening times, which are liable to change without notice.

Readers' Guide

◆ **Contact details:** These include the address, telephone number and website. You can enter the postcode to display a map of the location on Google and other map sites or, if you're driving, enter the postcode into your satnav.

◆ **Opening hours (where applicable):** These can change at short notice, therefore you should confirm by telephone or check the website before travelling, particularly over Christmas/New Year and on bank holidays, when many venues are closed. Many venues open daily, while some open only on weekdays, at weekends or on just a few days a week (and may have limited business or visiting hours). Some venues are only open by appointment or tickets must be purchased in advance.

◆ **Transport:** The nearest tube or rail station is listed, although in some cases it may involve a lengthy walk. You can also travel to most venues by bus and to some by river ferry. Venues outside central London are usually best reached by car, although parking can be difficult or impossible in some areas. Most venues don't provide parking, particularly in central London, and even parking nearby can be a problem (and very expensive). If you need to travel by car, check the local parking facilities beforehand (or take a taxi).

◆ **Prices:** Prices are liable to change and are intended only as a guide. Many venues – such as museums, galleries, parks, gardens and places of worship – offer free entry. We have provided a price guide for cafés, restaurants and hotels.

Disabled Access

Many historic public and private buildings don't provide wheelchair access or provide wheelchair access to the ground floor only. Wheelchairs are provided at some venues, although users may need assistance. Most museums, galleries and public buildings have a WC, although it may not be wheelchair accessible. Contact venues directly if you have specific requirements. The Disabled Go website (disabledgo.com) provides more in-depth access information for some destinations.

Contents

Introduction

There are great world cities – from classical capitals to modern metropolises – and then there's London. One of the oldest settlements in the Western world, its history stretches back to the Bronze Age, through Roman rule and the Norman Conquest, the machinations of the Middle Ages and the inventiveness of the Industrial Revolution, through to the Swinging Sixties and the new Millennium. London is the yardstick by which other cities are measured. It has the most astonishing ability to reinvent itself, always staying one step ahead of the pack, a magnet for creatives – be they writers or artists, designers or thinkers – and a melting pot of cultures from around the globe. New York may be hip, Paris may be chic, but London is surely the Capital of Cool.

The largest city in Europe, Greater London covers over 610mi² (1,580km²) with a population of 8.6 million. It's Britain's seat of government, the home of the Royal Family, the UK's commercial, cultural and sporting centre, Europe's leading financial market, the 'capital' of the English-speaking world; and a world leader in architecture, art, fashion, food, music, publishing, film and television.

London is also Europe's most culturally diverse city and one of the most cosmopolitan in the world; one in three Londoners (some 3 million people) were born outside the UK, hailing from all corners of the globe, particularly Europe and the Commonwealth countries of Africa, Asia and the West Indies. To add to this cultural potpourri, a phenomenal

20 million tourists swell London's population each year.

In creating this book we decided that the best way to illustrate London's cool credentials was to illustrate the very best that the city has to offer across a wide range of interests. So we've bar-hopped and dined, shopped and supped, boogied and bartered, and even gone for the burn in order to sample the city's best attractions. These include the coolest cocktail bars, smartest hotels, cosiest cafes and most atmospheric pubs, as well as restaurants that truly celebrate food and shops that redefine the art of retail therapy. Add to these the most exclusive members' clubs, hi-tech temples to fitness

and celebrity hotspots, and you have an idea of where we're going. And to take in some of London's more traditional pleasures we've included magnificent museums and awesome art galleries, breathtaking buildings, glorious churches and a swathe of tranquil green spaces that make London one of the greenest capitals in the world.

Some names are instantly recognisable – from the British Museum to the Shard – while others may surprise, and all are among the very best that London offers – and are therefore, by definition, among the very best in the world. We trust that you'll enjoy exploring them and that you'll agree that London – at its best – is truly unbeatable.

Welcome to the Big Smoke!

David Hampshire
April 2017

1.
Bars

London has always been a great place to let your hair down and has a dynamic bar scene that will satisfy the most discerning drinker. It's one of the most exciting cities in the world in which to eat, drink and be merry – in 2016, London had no fewer than eight of the world's 50 best bars according to Drinks International (www.worlds50bestbars.com), tipping New York into second place.

From opulent West End hotel bars to trendy South Bank speakeasies, Camden's cool indie destinations to super-hip hang outs in Shoreditch, London's bar scene offers a wealth of choice. They include designer cocktail lounges and champagne bars, glamorous piano bars, rooftop bars with panoramic views and edgy bohemian basement bars inspired by America's prohibition era, where fashionable Londoners gather in clandestine subterranean drinking dens, secreted behind unmarked doors and unassuming entrances. Along with cocktails – from classic to cutting edge – most bars offer tasty snacks or even full-blown gourmet meals, great music (DJs and live), cabaret and burlesque evenings; some even offer cocktail masterclasses so you can learn how to mix your own.

Whatever your budget or taste, our selection of the city's coolest and trendiest bars – and top-flight mixologists – will ensure that you're supping in some of the coolest places on the planet.

69 Colebrooke Row

Though named after its address – and also known by its tongue-in-cheek nickname of the 'Bar with No Name' – 69 has impressive cocktail credentials, including being consistently rated one of the world's best bars by Drinks International. It's a sister venue of the Zetter Townhouse (see page 123), and the man who mixes the cocktails here is the dapper, award-winning Tony Conigliaro. Opened in mid-2009, this renowned bar occupies a small intimate venue tucked away behind an anonymous exterior. Both cosy and elegant, the décor takes second billing to the drinks, which are the stars of the show.

The cocktail list is concise but well conceived and the drinks are clever combinations which leave you wanting

more. Most house cocktails are priced at £10.50 and served by smartly turned-out staff who know their stuff and are big on old-school charm. Another nice touch is the hand-written bills. You can also drink wine or beer, but why on earth would you in this cocktail connoisseurs' Mecca?

If you want to learn more about what makes the perfect cocktail, there are regular masterclasses, some hosted by Tony, costing £40 a head (see website for details).

69 Colebrooke Row, N1 8AA (07540-528593; www.69colebrookerow. com; Angel tube; Sun-Wed 5pm-midnight, Thu 5pm-1am, Fri-Sat 5pm-2am).

The American Bar

The American Bar on the Savoy Hotel's first floor evokes the roaring '20s, the so-called golden era of cocktails. It's an impressive venue – ranked 2nd in the world's 50 best bars 2016 by Drinks International – with understated Art Deco styling, elegant curves and Terry O'Neill photographic portraits on the walls, while a tuxedoed pianist plays American jazz to add to the ambience.

The Savoy Cocktail Book, published by Savoy barman Harry Craddock in the '30s, remains the cocktail mixologist's bible, and the position of head bartender here remains one of the hospitality world's most prestigious appointments. The Savoy is also home to the equally glamorous Beaufort Bar.

American Bar, Savoy Hotel, 100 Strand, WC2R 0EU (020-7836 4343; www.fairmont.com/savoy-london/dining/americanbar; Charing Cross tube/rail; Mon-Sat 11.30am-midnight, Sun noon-midnight).

Aqua Spirit

Part of a bar and restaurant complex (serving Japanese and Spanish cuisine) at the top of what used to be Dickens and Jones store, Aqua Spirit is a glamorous cocktail bar with a wonderful roof terrace, making it one of London's most desirable places to enjoy a drink on a warm summer evening.

The inside space is chic and sleek with a round bar offering a choice of some 30 cocktails, while the terrace has a wooden floor, comfortable chairs and panoramic views. Bookings aren't accepted for the terrace, so arrive early if you want a seat. Views vary depending on where you sit, and may include the BT Tower, Liberty department store and the London Eye.

Aqua Spirit, 240 Regent St, W1B 3BR, entrance 30 Argyll St (020-7478 0545; http://aquaspirit. co.uk; Oxford Circus tube; Mon-Sat noon-1am, Sun noon-10.30pm).

The Artesian Bar

Rated the world's best bar for four consecutive years (from 2012-2015) by Drinks International, the Artesian is one of London's most sumptuous watering holes – a triumph of classic-meets-contemporary design – in one of the city's grandest five star hotels. Recently updated by the noted David Collins Studio, it blends Victorian opulence – marble bar, embroidered napkins and mirrors – with modern magnificence: purple, leather-effect upholstery, ornate wood panelling and an extravagant 'Chinese Chippendale' centrepiece, as the pagoda-like back bar is called.

Rum is a speciality here, with around 50 on offer, which the Artesian claims is London's largest selection, plus an extensive champagne list. There's an excellent selection of inventive cocktails – as you'd expect from a former winner of Tales of the Cocktail's 'World's Best Cocktail Menu' (https://talesofthecocktail.com) – and the Artesian also prides itself on its gourmet bar food and faultless yet friendly service that makes everyone feel special.

The dress code is smart-casual and the location, opposite Broadcasting House, means you might see or hear the odd familiar face or voice. It isn't a cheap date, but neither is it ruinously expensive considering it's one of the world's best bars.

Artesian, Langham Hotel, 1C Portland Pl, Regent St, W1B 1JA (020-7636 1000; www.artesian-bar. co.uk; Oxford Circus tube; Mon-Sat 11am-2am, Sun 11am-midnight).

Bar Termini

One of the city's smallest bars, bar Termini is cocktail alchemist Tony Conigliaro's (of 69 Colebrooke Row fame) and coffee maestro Marco Arrigo's homage to Rome's Termini train station. The bar's favourite tipples include the Spritz Termini (a turbo-charged Aperol Spritz with gin, rhubarb cordial and a champagne-pickled almond), the Marsala Martini (gin, dry vermouth, Marsala Dolce, dry vermouth and almond bitters) and a selection of superb negronis.

There are also bar snacks.

The tiny bar seats just 25, although you can stand (Italian-style) if you order a single 'espresso al bar'. Bookings (after 5pm) are limited to just 60 minutes – so you don't miss your train!

Bar Termini, 7 Old Compton Street, W1D 5JE (07860-945018; www.bar-termini.com; Leicester Sq tube; Mon-Thu 10am-11.30pm, Fri-Sat 10am-1am, Sun 11am-10.30pm).

Beach Blanket Babylon

Spread over three floors of a former Victorian warehouse, Beach Blanket Babylon in Shoreditch is a bar-cum-gallery that 'encapsulates the bohemian decadence of Cool Britannia'. The décor is a blend of boho chic and French country château, with gilded wallpaper, over-the-top furniture and glitzy ornaments.

The cocktail lounge can accommodate 300 and the restaurant seats another 150, and there's also a large gallery space for exhibitions and special events. The basement cocktail lounge (there are two) is exotically decked out with patterned flock wallpaper and 18th-century and Art Deco decoration, so dress accordingly.

Beach Blanket Babylon, 19-23 Bethnal Green Rd, E1 6LA (020-7749 3540; www.beachblanket. co.uk; Shoreditch High St rail; Mon-Thu 5pm-midnight, Fri-Sat noon-1am, Sun noon-midnight).

The Booking Office

This hotel bar (and restaurant) has the distinct advantage of being housed in one of London's architectural highlights, St Pancras Station, where the former grand station café is now the Booking Office bar in the five-star St Pancras Renaissance London Hotel (formerly the Midland Grand Hotel, opened in 1873).

The bar echoes the building's cathedral-like Victorian splendour, with plenty of seating from which to admire the original arched windows, ribbed vaulting and intricate, decorative brickwork. Drinks are served from a 95ft long bar, where the speciality is (not surprisingly) cocktails. The Renaissance is also home to the equally impressive Gilbert Scott bar.

Booking Office Bar, St Pancras Renaissance Hotel, NW1 2AR (020-7841 3566; www. stpancraslondon.com/en/restaurant-bars/ booking-office; King's Cross tube/rail; Mon-Wed 6.30am-1am, Thu-Sat 6.30am-late, Sun 6.30am-midnight).

Calloph Callay

Set on a cobbled side street and loosely Lewis Carroll-themed – named after an expression in his nonsense poem *Jabberwocky* – award-winning Callooh Callay in hipster Shoreditch is one of the world's best cocktail bars, designed with imagination and flair. The venue is split into three areas – the Bar, the Lounge and the Upstairs Bar – and you enter through a 'wardrobe' (shouldn't that be a looking glass?) to get to the main bar area, which has a long counter and low purple seating.

Cocktails are the drink of choice here and there's an interesting range to choose from, as well as imaginative bar snacks. There are DJs at weekends and cocktail masterclasses, too.

Callooh Callay, 65 Rivington St, EC2A 3AY (020-7739 4781; www.calloohcallaybar.com; Old St tube/rail; daily 6pm-1am).

The Connaught Bar

The more famous of this landmark Mayfair hotel's two bars (the other is the Coburg), the Connaught was ranked 4th in the world's 50 best bars in 2016. It's a dramatic Art Deco drinking den (designed by David Collins) in leather, marble and metal, using a palette of lilac and pink, pistachio and silver.

Cosy and understated, with subtle lighting and excellent service, cocktails are the speciality here – it's particularly noted for its perfect martinis, which are gently stirred, never shaken (sorry Mr Bond). The exceptional (if expensive) bar effortlessly manages to combine 21st-century style with considerable Old World charm, the kind of place where you're made to feel special by the friendly professional staff.

The Connaught Bar, The Connaught, Carlos Pl, W1K 2AL (020-7314 3419; www.the-connaught. co.uk/mayfair-bars/connaught-bar; Bond St tube; Mon-Sat 4pm-1am, Sun 4pm-midnight).

The Crazy Bear

It's evident that lots of money has been lavished on the sumptuous, dimly-lit Crazy Bear cocktail bar in Fitzrovia, which sits beneath a restaurant serving modern Chinese, Japanese and Thai cuisine. The bar is most definitely plush – even the loos are extravagantly done, replete with crystal and mirrors aplenty – but it isn't just about show.

The friendly bar staff mix a superb cocktail, albeit a pricey one. It's popular and usually busy – a lot of diners from the excellent upstairs restaurant begin and end their evenings in the bar – so book if you wish to ensure somewhere to sit. You can also order dim sum and sushi in the bar.

The Crazy Bear, 26-28 Whitfield St, W1T 2RG (020-7631 0088; www.crazybeargroup.co.uk/ fitzrovia/bar; Goodge St tube; Tue-Wed noon-midnight, Thu-Sat noon-1am, Sun midday-midnight, Mon closed).

The Dandelyan Bar

It's unusual to find a swanky cocktail bar south of the river, but the Dandelyan Bar at the Mondrian Hotel (see page 116) is highly rated (3rd in the world's 50 best bars 2016 by Drinks International) and visually exciting, with startling candy purple leather banquettes, velvet armchairs, green marble bar, parquet flooring and panoramic Thames' views.

Created by award-winning mixologist Ryan Chetiyawardana, Dandelyan serves both refined interpretations of the classics and delectable innovative creations – such as the Concrete Sazerac (cognac, fermented Peychaud's bitters and absinthe, filtered through concrete) – taking inspiration from British and international botanicals.

Dandelyan Bar, Mondrian Hotel, 20 Upper Ground, SE1 9PD (020-3747 1000; www. morganshotelgroup.com/mondrian/mondrian-london/eat-drink/Dandelyan; Southwark tube; Mon-Wed 4pm-1am, Thu 4pm-2am, Fri-Sat noon-2am, Sun noon-12.30am).

Discount Suit Company

A cool, clandestine, subterranean bar in Shoreditch with a great vibe, the Discount Suit Company – occupying a former tailor's stockroom from which it takes its name – is a laid-back, informal drinking den. The 'décor' is candlelight and exposed brickwork, Victorian floorboards and (very) low ceiling beams – duck unless you're under 5ft tall.

DSC focuses on classic recipes and a changing menu of bargain signature cocktails such as Dark Cloud (rye whiskey, Chamberyzette, chocolate tea syrup and lemon) and Herbal Habit (Cocchi Americano, green Chartreuse, Benedictine, lime and mint). There are also tasty Neal's Yard cheese boards and cool sounds (a DJ visits some days).

Discount Suit Company, 29A Wentworth St, E1 7TB (020-7247 8755; www.discountsuitcompany. co.uk; Aldgate/Liverpool St tube; Mon-Thu 5pm-midnight, Fri-Sat 2pm-1am, Sun 5-11pm).

The Experimental Cocktail Club

This London outpost of Paris' Experimental Cocktail Club is a buzzing two-floor, speakeasy-style bar secreted behind a battered black door in Chinatown. Opulent and cosy, the cool bar features exposed brick, subtle lighting, mirrored walls and some great sounds. Cocktails are, of course, the thing to drink here (there's also a good wine list), covering the classics as well as more off-the-wall mixes – appropriate given the venue's name – which are invariably brilliantly creative, served by friendly, knowledgeable staff (and in glasses, not test tubes!). Good bar snacks, too.

You can reserve a table by email (reservation@chinatownecc.com), although half the seats are reserved for walk-ins.

The Experimental Cocktail Club, 13A Gerrard St, W1D 5PS (020-7434 3559; www.chinatownecc. com; Leicester Sq tube; Mon-Sat 6pm-3am, Sun 6pm-midnight).

The Gibson

Paying homage to a cocktail (gin and vermouth garnished with a pickled onion) created in the 1900s, the Gibson is an Edwardian time machine. The lovechild of two of the city's most respected bartenders, Marian Beke (ex-Nightjar) and Rusty Cerven (ex-Connaught), the intimate '20s-themed cocktail bar near Old St (opened in 2015) is highly rated, serving killer cocktails.

While the Gibson (cocktail) is the star – in various guises – there's a wealth of original creations on offer on the ever-evolving menu, all theatrically presented with flamboyant garnishes (pickles are a popular theme) that will leave your taste buds tingling and yearning for more. There's also live music.

The Gibson, 44 Old Street, EC1V 9AQ (020-7608 2774; www.thegibsonbar.london; Old St tube; Mon-Thu 5pm-1am, Fri-Sat 5pm-2am, closed Sun).

Happiness Forgets

One of London's, and the world's, coolest bars, Happiness Forgets – the name is taken from Burt Bacharach's song, *Loneliness Remembers what Happiness Forgets* – was opened in 2010 by Ali Burgess and is still very much an 'in' place. Indeed, it was ranked 10th in the world's 50 best bars 2016 by Drinks International.

It's a tiny, dimly-lit basement bar, with hints of the speakeasy about it, lit by the warm glow from '50s lamps and candles, while dark walls and wooden floorboards add to the subterranean atmosphere. It's relaxed and friendly with a nicely mixed crowd, including both local creatives and business suits, but somehow avoids being yet another den of Shoreditch pretentiousness. The drinks are predictably great with a good choice of beer and wine, but cocktails are the house speciality; we recommend the Perfect Storm (dark rum, honey, lemon, freshly squeezed ginger juice and plum brandy). The website sums HF up nicely: 'High end cocktails, low rent basement,' along with 'Great cocktails, no wallies'.

Bookings can be made by email (reservations@happinessforgets.com) for parties of two to six. Now with a little sister, Original Sin, in Stoke Newington.

Happiness Forgets, 8-9 Hoxton Sq, N1 6NU (020-7613 0325; www.happinessforgets.com; Old St tube/rail; daily 5-11pm).

Hawksmoor Spitalfields Bar

The original of a small chain of steakhouse-bars located just down the road from Nicholas Hawksmoor's elegant Christ Church, Spitalfields – hence the name. The cellar bar boasts stunning décor, including a copper bar and wall panels, and turquoise Victorian glazed bricks.

In endeavouring to create London's best cocktail bars, Hawksmoor have 'scoured their library of long out-of-print cocktail books to resurrect some great long-lost classics' and their skilled bartenders have also worked their magic to invent a few of their own to add to the extensive list. There's a great bar menu, too (try the shortrib nuggets or lobster roll).

Hawksmoor Spitalfields Bar, 157B Commercial St, E1 6BJ (020-7426 4856; www.thehawksmoor. com/spitalfieldsbar; Shoreditch High St rail; Mon-Thu 5.30-11pm, Fri 5.30pm-1am, Sat noon-1am, closed Sun).

The Lobby Bar

Situated in the part of London where the City meets the West End, the beautiful Lobby Bar at trendy One Aldwych hotel attracts both financial and creative types. It was named one of the top five hotel bars in the world by the *Sunday Telegraph* and is a place to take somebody you want to impress: an ultra-stylish bar with pillars, ceiling-high windows, striking artwork, huge flower displays and a polished limestone floor.

There's a wide choice of drinks, with well-made cocktails and an extensive choice of champagne, wine and beer, as well as an interesting bar menu, including sharing platters – something for everyone.

The Lobby Bar, One Aldwych, WC2B 4BZ (020-7300 1070; www.onealdwych.com/food-drink/the-lobby-bar; Covent Gdn tube; Mon-Fri 8am-midnight, Sat 9am-midnight, Sun 9am-10.30pm).

Mark's Bar

Part of the stable of entrepreneurial chef Mark Hix (his restaurant HIX Soho is on the ground floor), Mark's Bar in Brewer St is a stylish, speakeasy-like basement venue. A long zinc bar, tin ceiling and Chesterfield sofas make for a dramatic room with a lovely atmosphere.

Some thought has gone into the drinks menu, which includes an impressive cocktail list (many based on true-Brit recipes from years gone by) and a well-chosen selection of wine, champagne and beer. The licence dictates that drinkers must order food, which is no hardship as there are great bar snacks and you can also choose from the restaurant menu.

Mark's Bar, 66-70 Brewer St, W1F 9UP (020-7292 3518; www.marksbar.co.uk; Piccadilly Circus tube; Mon-Sat noon-1am, Sun noon-midnight).

The Mayor of Scaredy Cat Town

Yet another modern-day speakeasy – possibly the best in town and certainly the best-named – the Mayor of Scaredy Cat Town is secreted beneath the Breakfast Club in Spitalfields. The entrance is via a Smeg fridge door and the amusing kitsch doesn't stop there, with 'No Heavy Petting' posters and cat bowls on the floor. (You exit via the bathrooms to ensure the bar remains a 'secret'.)

Inside there's a moodily-lit cocktail bar with exposed brickwork and wood, some great music and a wide choice of good-value creative cocktails, such as Ricky's Cucumber (Portobello Road gin, cucumber, lime, matcha powder, soda and sugar).

Mayor of Scaredy Cat Town, 12-16 Artillery Ln, E1 7LS (020-7078 9639; www. themayorofscaredycattown.com; Liverpool St tube/rail; Mon-Tue 5pm-midnight, Wed-Thu 3.30pm-midnight, Fri 3pm-midnight, Sat noon-midnight, Sun noon-10.30pm).

Nightjar

The anonymous entrance to this stylish Shoreditch basement bar – rated number 19 in the world's 50 best bars by Drinks International – sits incongruously between two cafeterias. Reminiscent of a '20s speakeasy, Nightjar specialises in cocktails, cabaret and jazz, and has a debonair atmosphere, describing itself as 'a hidden slice of old school glamour'. The interior is all dark wood, dim lighting and black leather booths – very much a place for grown-ups.

Cocktails are the thing here, both ancient and modern – some recipes date back to 1600 while others include unusual

flavourings such as durian fruit, plankton, marigold, tobacco sugar, squid ink and bee pollen syrup – and very good they are, too. The cocktail menu (around 50) is split into Pre-Prohibition, Prohibition, Post-War (mostly tiki) and Signature drinks. Beer, spirits and wine are also available, while bar snacks include cheese, charcuterie and tapas.

Nightjar is, not surprisingly, very popular and has a no-standing policy, therefore booking is essential (well in advance for weekends). There's vintage live music from the cocktail era ('20s-'40s) from around 9pm Tue-Sat. Entrance is free on Mondays and Tuesdays but there's a door charge (£5-8) from Wednesday to Saturdays. Nightjar now has an equally impressive sister bar, the Oriole.

Nightjar, 129 City Rd, EC1V 1JB (020-7253 4101; www.barnightjar.com; Old St tube/rail; Sun-Wed 6pm-1am, Thu 6pm-2am, Fri-Sat 6pm-3am).

Purl

Located in the basement of a Georgian house in Marylebone, super-cool Purl – named for an old English drink of warm ale, gin, wormwood and spices – is a relaxed and unfussy place, with plenty of individual seating areas, leather furniture, brick walls and a low vaulted ceiling.

Beer and wine are available, but it's the well-made, inventive cocktails and the associated theatre of making and serving them that's the main draw. As the website states, Purl serves drinks 'that satisfy on a multi-sensory level, using aroma, fogs, airs, foam, food, bespoke service-wear and liquid nitrogen to bring the drink to life and transport the guest to another place or time'. Booking essential.

Purl, 50-54 Blandford St, W1U 7HX (020-7935 0835, www.purl-london.com; Bond St tube; Mon-Thu 5-11.30pm, Fri-Sat 5pm-midnight, closed Sun).

Scarfes Bar

Named after the noted British satirical artist and cartoonist, Gerald Scarfe – whose work adorns the bar – the opulent and refined Scarfes Bar in the Rosewood Hotel is an atmospheric combination of drawing room, gentlemen's club and library, featuring a roaring fire (in winter), low-key lighting, a beautiful long bar, cosy velvet armchairs and shelves over-flowing with antique books.

The bar specialises in whiskies – including over 200 single malts – and sloe gin, plus a few craft beers, although it's the creative and expertly-made cocktails that draw the crowds. Live music and delicious Indian food and bar snacks from Palash Mitra add to its allure.

Scarfes Bar, Rosewood Hotel, 252 High Holborn, WC1V 7EN (020-3747 8670; http://scarfesbar. com; Holborn tube; Mon-Sat noon-late, Sun 3pm-late).

Trailer Happiness

This Notting Hill basement bar describes itself as a 'lounge bar, den and kitchen' and a 'retro-sexy haven of cosmopolitan kitsch and faded trailer park glamour'. However, it doesn't take itself seriously – the décor is a mixture of palm trees, bright colours and '60s art – which is a healthy

change in this part of town. The nicely tacky interior aims for lo-fi glamour and there are DJs Thu-Sat, so it isn't a typical cocktail bar. The drinks are excellent, with classic and contemporary cocktails spread across three menus: House Favourites, Tiki Classics and Homage Drinks. It's a relaxed, affordable venue with a happy, friendly crowd, so it's hardly surprising that it's popular.

Trailer Happiness, 177 Portobello Rd, W11 2DY (020-7041 9833; www.trailerhappiness.com; Ladbroke Grove tube; Sun-Wed 5pm-midnight, Thu 5-12.30am, Fri-Sat 5pm-1am).

The Worship Street Whistling Shop

The sister bar to Purl in Marylebone, the award-winning Worship Street Whistling Shop – historically a spirit shop, especially a secret and illicit one – has opted for all-out Victoriana; its décor has a distinctly Dickensian air with Chesterfield sofas, gas lamps and staff in period clothing.

Drinks at The Whistling Shop (like those at Purl) are a cunning blend of historic and modern. Its mixologists experiment with creating flavour combinations using a range of elements and equipment more at home in a chemistry lab (blame Heston Blumenthal!), allowing you to sample unusual cocktails alongside barrel-aged spirit infusions based on gin, rum and more unexpected ingredients.

Worship Street Whistling Shop, 63 Worship St, EC2A 2DU (020-7247 0015; www.whistlingshop. com; Old St tube/rail; Mon-Tue 5pm-midnight, Wed-Thu 5pm-1am, Fri-Sat 5pm-2am, closed Sun).

2.

Buildings & Structures

London has one of the most recognisable skylines in the world. Its iconic buildings range from the venerable – the Houses of Parliament, Buckingham Palace and Tower Bridge – to the strikingly modern, such as 30 St Mary Axe (aka the Gherkin) and the Shard. The latter are the result of a boom in high-rise building since the '90s, which has taken London's previously relatively low-rise skyline – which was intentionally designed to protect the views of St Paul's Cathedral – to soaring new heights.

Unlike many cities, London isn't characterised by any particular architectural style. It has accumulated its buildings over a long period of time, although relatively few predate the Great Fire of 1666 (exceptions include the Tower of London, Westminster Abbey and Banqueting House), and many more were destroyed during the Second World War, which saw the loss of many historic churches. Among the great architects who have left their mark on the city are Sir Christopher Wren, Sir John Soane, John Nash, Sir Charles Barry and, more recently, Lord Norman Foster, Lord Richard Rogers and Renzo Piano.

In addition to the buildings and structures featured in this chapter, many more feature elsewhere in the book, including St Paul's Cathedral, Westminster Abbey, the Natural History Museum, the St Pancras Renaissance Hotel and the Tate Modern, to name just a few.

Banqueting House

This noble structure is the only surviving part of the Palace of Whitehall. The palace was the main London residence of English monarchs from 1530 and grew to become the largest in Europe – larger even than the Vatican and Versailles – until 1698, when all except Inigo Jones' Banqueting House was destroyed by fire. The surviving building, which dates from 1622, is significant in the history of English architecture, being the first designed in the neo-classical style that would transform the country.

Its main attraction is its richly-painted ceiling, a masterpiece by the Antwerp-based artist and diplomat Peter Paul Rubens, commissioned by King Charles I who (ironically) was beheaded on a scaffold erected outside the hall in 1649.

Banqueting House, Whitehall, SW1A 2ER (020-3166 6154/5; www.hrp.org.uk/banquetinghouse; Westminster/Embankment tube; daily 10am-5pm; adults £6.60, concessions £5.50, under-16s free).

Barbican Estate

A prominent example of British Brutalist concrete architecture, encompassing Europe's largest arts and conference venue, the Barbican Estate is a vast 40-acre development containing three residential tower blocks, built between 1965 and 1976 and designed by architects Chamberlin, Powell and Bon. Designated a site of special architectural interest for its scale, cohesion and ambition, the design – a concrete ziggurat – is controversial and divides opinion: it was voted 'London's ugliest building' in an unofficial poll in 2003.

The Barbican Arts Centre (see page 153) stages a comprehensive range of art, music, theatre, dance, film and creative learning events. There's also a library, restaurants, gardens and a glorious conservatory.

Barbican Centre, Silk St, EC2Y 8DS (020-7638 4141; www.barbican.org.uk; Barbican tube; Mon-Sat 9am-11pm, Sun noon-11pm; free).

Buildingham Palace

The official London residence of British monarchs since 1837, Buckingham Palace stands in splendid isolation at the top of the Mall, one of the most iconic sights in the capital. Until fairly recently the only way to see inside was by invitation – to a banquet, investiture or one of the famous garden parties – but since 1993 the state rooms have been open to the public in summer when the Queen and her family decamp to Balmoral in Scotland. You can also visit the Queen's Gallery and the Royal Mews year round.

The Palace was originally built as a townhouse for the Duke of Buckingham in 1705. It was purchased in 1761 by George III as a residence for his wife Queen Charlotte, but it was their son George IV who commissioned John Nash to transform it into a palace at huge expense. It became the principle royal residence in 1837 when the young Queen Victoria moved in and was further extended during the 19th century. Today, the palace has 775 rooms, including 19 state rooms, 52 royal and guest bedrooms, 188 staff bedrooms, 92 offices and 78 bathrooms.

Buckingham Palace, SW1A 1AA (020-7766 7300; www.royalcollection.org.uk/visit/the-state-rooms-buckingham-palace; St James's Pk tube; see website for visitor options, times and fees).

The Charterhouse (Sutton's Hospital)

Hidden away in the City is one of London's most beautiful and historic buildings, the Charterhouse, formally known as Sutton's Hospital in Charterhouse. The site was once the location of London's largest plague pit, where around 50,000 victims of the Black Death were buried in 1348. It also housed a Carthusian monastery, founded in 1371 by Sir Walter de Manny and the Bishop of London, and dissolved by Henry VIII in 1537.

The Charterhouse was purchased in 1611 by Thomas Sutton (1532-1611), an Elizabethan merchant and adventurer, who endowed a hospital on the site. When Sutton died the greater part of his vast fortune was bequeathed to maintain a chapel, the hospital and school – the latter moved to Surrey in 1872. The hospital – or almshouse, which is still in operation – was

a home for gentlemen pensioners, housing up to 80 men (now 40), and the school catered for 40 'poor' scholars.

Today, Charterhouse is part of the campus of Queen Mary, University of London, and lodgings are still provided for gentlemen who fall on hard times. Pre-booked tours (£10) of this medieval gem are organised on selected days.

The Charterhouse, Sutton's Hospital, Charterhouse Sq, EC1M 6AN (020-7253 9503; www.thecharterhouse. org/tours; Barbican tube; tours on selected days – see website for information).

Dennis Severs' House

One of London's most singular attractions, Dennis Severs' House has been designed to create an atmosphere redolent of the 18th century and paint a picture of what life was like then. It's the brainchild of an American artist, Dennis Severs, who purchased the house in the '70s when the old Huguenot district of Spitalfields was rundown and little valued.

Each of the ten rooms reflects a different era of the house's past, a snapshot of the life of the families who 'lived' here between 1724 and 1914. Dennis Severs died in 1999, but the house has been preserved and is open for tours. The candlelit night-time tours are the most atmospheric.

Dennis Severs' House, 18 Folgate St, Spitalfields, E1 6BX (020-7247 4013; www. dennissevershouse.co.uk; Liverpool St tube/rail; see website for visiting times and fees).

Eltham Palace

Initially a moated manor house set in extensive parkland, Eltham Palace was given to Edward II in 1305 and was a royal residence from the 14th to 16th centuries – Henry VIII spent his childhood there.

The current building (now owned by English Heritage) dates from the '30s, when Sir Stephen and Lady Courtauld restored the Great Hall, which boasts England's third-largest hammer-beam roof, gave it a minstrels' gallery, and incorporated it into a sumptuous home with a striking interior in a variety of Art Deco styles. Among many notable features are Lady Courtauld's gold-plated mosaic bathroom and the stunning circular entrance hall, the work of the Swedish designer Rolf Engströmer.

Eltham Palace, Court Yd, Eltham, SE9 5QE (020-8294 2548; www.english-heritage.org.uk/ daysout/properties/eltham-palace-and-gardens; Eltham or Mottingham rail; see website for visiting times and fees).

Fulham Palace

Secreted in a tree-enclosed haven in west London, with lovely gardens and a tranquil Thameside location, Fulham Palace is one of the city's oldest and most historically significant buildings. It was the country home of the Bishops of London for over 900 years, and excavations have revealed several former large-scale buildings and evidence of settlements dating back to Roman and Neolithic times.

Much of the surviving palace building (Grade I listed) dates from 1495 and encompasses a variety of different building styles and ages, while the extensive gardens contain a wealth of international plant species. The Palace also contains a shop, a museum, a contemporary art gallery and a café.

Fulham Palace, Bishop's Ave, Fulham, SW6 6EA (020-7736 3233; www.fulhampalace.org; Putney Br tube or Putney rail; see website for opening times; free).

The Gherkin

Generally regarded as London's finest contemporary building – and one of its most distinctive – 30 St Mary Axe (its official name) is sometimes called the Swiss Re Building after its main occupier, although it's much better known by its nickname, the Gherkin. A triumph of architecture-as-sculpture, it was designed by Norman Foster and Arup engineers and won its creators the Stirling Prize in 2004.

As visitors crane their necks to take in the 591ft, 41-floor tower, they sometimes ignore the building's entrance, approached across a landscaped plaza bordered by the unusual Arcadian Garden, described as a 'poem and artwork'. Sadly, the interior isn't open to the public, unless you're a member of Searcy's, the Gherkin (see page 91).

30 St Mary Axe, EC3A 8EP (020-7071 5000; www.30stmaryaxe.info; Aldgate tube or Liverpool Street tube/rail).

Hampton Court Palace

A vast royal palace covering 6 acres on the River Thames, Hampton Court Palace (Grade I listed) was built in 1514 for Cardinal Thomas Wolsey – Lord Chancellor and favourite of Henry VIII – but was appropriated by the King in 1529 when Wolsey fell from favour. Henry made it his main London residence and greatly enlarged it. Further extensive rebuilding by William III in the following century (intended to rival Versailles) was halted in 1694, leaving the palace in two distinct contrasting architectural styles: domestic Tudor and Baroque.

Today, it remains a royal palace – one of only two surviving palaces previously occupied by Henry VIII (the other is St James's) – but hasn't been inhabited by the British royal family since the 18th century, when George II was resident (his son,

Astronomical clock

George III, never set foot there as king). It's maintained by an independent charity, Historic Royal Palaces, and is a major tourist attraction. It receives no funding from the government or the crown, hence the eye-watering admission prices, but remains good value. The palace's Home Park is the site of the annual Hampton Court Palace Festival and the RHS Hampton Court Palace Flower Show.

Hampton Court Palace, East Molesey, KT8 9AU (020-3166 6000; www.hrp.org.uk/hamptoncourtpalace; Hampton Court rail; see website for opening times and fees).

Houses of Parliament

The Houses of Parliament – or Palace of Westminster to give it its formal name – is London's most iconic building and one of the most famous buildings in the world, containing the two Houses of Parliament:

the Commons and the House of Lords. It was constructed between 1840 and 1870 and replaced an earlier medieval palace destroyed by fire in 1834 (the surviving Westminster Hall, chapel of St Mary Undercroft Chapel and the Cloisters of St Stephen's were incorporated into the 'new' Palace).

Designed by architects Sir Charles Barry and Augustus Pugin (who was responsible for the beautiful interiors) – neither of whom lived to see the Palace finished – in the perpendicular Gothic style, it contains 1,100 rooms formed around two courtyards and covers an area of eight acres with an impressive 870ft (266m) river frontage. Standing proud of the main building is the famous clock tower (Elizabeth Tower), home of the bell affectionately known as Big Ben, although nowadays this name is used to refer to the clock.

Tours of Parliament take visitors into both the Commons' and Lords' Chambers and historic Westminster Hall. UK residents can also book a tour (via their MP) to climb Elizabeth Tower and see Big Ben up close.

Houses of Parliament, Westminster, SW1A 0AA (020-7219 3000 or 020-7219 4114 for tickets; www.parliament.uk/visiting; Westminster tube; see website for visiting times).

Inns of Court

London's four Inns of Court – Lincoln's Inn, Inner Temple, Middle Temple and Gray's Inn – date back to the 14th century and anyone wishing to train as a barrister for the Bar must join one of them. Each is a large complex covering several acres, with a great hall, libraries, a chapel, chambers and gardens, reminiscent of an Oxbridge college.

The Inns are oases of calm amid the hustle and bustle of the City, with quadrangles, lawns and plane trees, and are a delight to wander around, particularly at dusk when their gas lamps are being lit.

Inns of Court: Gray's Inn Rd, WC1; King's Bench Walk, EC4; Lincoln's Inn Fields, WC2; and Middle Temple Ln, EC4 (http://barcouncil. org.uk/about-the-bar/what-is-the-bar/inns-of-court; Temple or Chancery Ln tube; exterior unrestricted access, see website for tours).

Kensington Palace

Kensington Palace has been a Royal residence since 1689 and has a fascinating historical and archaeological heritage. Today it's home to Prince William and his wife Catherine (the Duke and Duchess of Cambridge) and other extended members of the Royal Family.

The Palace began life as a Jacobean mansion, built in the early 17th century for the Earl of Nottingham, and was purchased by William III and his wife Mary II in 1689. Sir Christopher Wren enlarged it by adding pavilions to each corner and also reoriented it to face Hyde Park. It's a fascinating building well worth a visit, as are the beautiful gardens, finishing with lunch or afternoon tea in the Orangery Restaurant.

Kensington Palace, Kensington Gardens, W8 4PX (020-3166 6000; www.hrp.org.uk/kensingtonpalace; High St Kensington/Queensway tube; see website for opening times and fees).

Lloyd's of London

Lloyd's is the world's specialist insurance market and the remarkable Lloyd's building is its HQ. The world's most famous name in insurance, Lloyd's isn't a company but a marketplace, where members join together as syndicates to insure risks. The world-famous Lloyd's building was designed by architect Richard Rogers and took eight years to build, being completed in 1986; it was granted Grade I listed building status in 2011 (the newest ever to achieve this accolade).

The amazing steel-clad, concrete-framed construction is unlike any of the traditional Portland stone edifices nearby and was an audacious high-tech project in a location where conservative attitudes to the built environment prevailed. It has its services on its façade (like the Pompidou Centre in Paris, also designed by Rogers), exposing its pipes, toilet pods, staircases and glass lifts to the rest of the

City of London and passers-by. The large clear floor plates, uncluttered by services, are connected by escalators to facilitate easy internal communication and natural light enters from all directions and from an atrium, which dominates the interior.

Today the Lloyd's building is universally recognised as one of the most significant of the modern era and is well worth a visit.

Lloyd's of London, One Lime St, EC3M 7HA (020-7327 1000; www.lloyds.com/lloyds/about-us/visiting-lloyds; Bank/Monument tube; see website for tours).

The London Eye

A giant Ferris wheel – strictly speaking it's a cantilevered observation wheel – on the south bank of the Thames, the (Coca-Cola) London Eye was designed by Marks Barfield Architects. It opened in March 2000 to celebrate the start of the new century

and quickly became one of the most iconic sights of the capital and one of the UK's most popular paid tourist attractions, with some 4 million visitors annually.

The wheel stands 443ft (135m) tall with a diameter of 394ft (120m) and is Europe's tallest observation wheel, with 32 10-tonne capsules each holding up to 25 people. On a clear day you can see for up to 25 miles (40km).

The London Eye, Riverside Building, County Hall, Westminster Bridge Rd, SE1 7PB (www. londoneye.com; Waterloo tube/rail; see website for opening times and fees).

Michelin House

Michelin House was designed by François Espinasse (a Michelin employee) as the UK headquarters of the Michelin Tyre Company, opening in 1911. Its exuberant stylistic individualism has been variously described as Art Nouveau, proto-Art Deco, Secessionist Functionalism and geometrical Classicism, featuring stained-glass windows depicting the 'Michelin Man' (Bibendum) and Parisian maps, ceramic tiles of famous racing cars, mosaic floors and decorative metalwork.

Today the building contains offices, a Conran shop, and the Bibendum Restaurant, along with the more informal Oyster Bar. It's well worth a visit to behold this amazing building – and the food's not bad either!

Michelin House, 81 Fulham Rd, SW3 6RD (www. bibendum.co.uk/the-building.html; S Kensington tube; see website for café/restaurant opening times).

The Monument

At 202ft (62m) high, this London landmark is the world's tallest isolated stone column. It was designed by Sir Christopher Wren and his friend the

scientist Dr Robert Hooke, and built between 1671 and 1677. The huge, fluted Doric column (made of Portland stone) commemorates the Great Fire of London (1666), and is topped by a drum and a flaming bronze urn symbolising the fire.

From the public viewing platform (160ft) you can enjoy a bird's-eye view of the City and further afield, but be warned: climbing the 311 steps isn't for the lazy, nervous or very unfit.

The Monument, junction of Monument St and Fish St Hill, EC3R 6DB (020-7626 2717; www. themonument.info; Monument tube; daily 9.30am to 5.30 or 6pm; adults £4, concessions £2.70, children under 16 £2).

Nelson's Column

Commemorating the death of Admiral Horatio Nelson (b. 1758) at the Battle of Trafalgar in 1805, Nelson's Column in Trafalgar Square was designed by William Railton and built between 1840 and 1843. Topped by an 18ft/5.5m sandstone statue of Nelson looking south towards the Admiralty, the column stands 170ft (50m) high.

The square pedestal at the foot of the Corinthian column is decorated with four 18ft^2 bas-relief bronze panels cast from captured French guns and depicting Nelson's famous victories at the Battles of Cape St Vincent, the Nile, Copenhagen and Trafalgar. The four bronze lions (by Sir Edwin Landseer) guarding the base of the column were added in 1867, 24 years after the statue was erected.

Nelson's Column, Trafalgar Sq, WC2N 5DN (www.london.gov.uk/about-us/our-building-and-squares/trafalgar-square; Charing Cross tube/ rail; free access 24 hours).

Old Royal Naval College

As the centrepiece of the Maritime Greenwich World Heritage Site, the classical buildings that collectively form the Old Royal Naval College (ORNC) were designed by some of England's most renowned architects and are considered to be amongst the finest in Europe.

The College is Sir Christopher Wren's twin-domed riverside masterpiece and one of London's most famous landmarks, incorporating the original (1694) Royal Hospital for Seamen (which became the Royal Naval College in 1873) and the magnificent Painted Hall and Chapel. However, most of the work was carried out by Nicholas Hawksmoor, overseen by Wren and assisted by John James, with the final blocks completed by Thomas Ripley between 1735 and 1751.

Old Royal Naval College, King William Walk, SE10 9NN (020-8269 4747; www.ornc.org; Cutty Sark DLR or Greenwich rail; 9 or 10am-5pm; free).

Royal Courts of Justice

The Grade I listed Royal Courts of Justice, commonly called the Law Courts, is a vast, imposing building housing the Courts of Appeal and the High Court of Justice of England and Wales. It's one of the last great wonders of Victorian neo-Gothic revival architecture, designed by George Edmund Street

RA (1824-1881), with imposing Portland stonework, beautiful mosaic marble floors, stunning stained glass windows, elaborate carvings and oak wood panelling.

Built in the 1870s and officially opened in 1882 by Queen Victoria, the finished building contained 35 million Portland stone bricks, over 3.5mi (5.6km) of corridors and some 1,000 clocks, many of which had to be wound by hand.

Royal Courts of Justice, The Strand, WC2A 2LL (07789-751248; www.justice.gov.uk/courts/rcj-rolls-building/rcj/tours; Temple tube; free access most days; see website for information about tours).

Royal Hospital Chelsea

The Royal Hospital Chelsea is a beautiful, redbrick (Grade I listed) building regarded as London's second-loveliest façade on the Thames (after Greenwich), while the attractive grounds have been the site of the celebrated Chelsea Flower Show since 1913.

The hospital was founded by Charles II for the 'succour and relief of veterans (dubbed 'Chelsea pensioners') broken by age and war', a purpose which it still serves to this day. Designed by Sir Christopher Wren and completed in 1692, the hospital was built around three courtyards and remains largely unchanged except for minor alterations by Robert Adam between 1765 and 1782, and the stables, which were added by Sir John Soane in 1814.

Royal Hospital Chelsea, Royal Hospital Rd, SW3 4SR (020-7881 5200; www.chelsea-pensioners. co.uk; Sloane Sq tube; free entry; see website for opening hours and tours).

Senate House

Designed by British architect Charles Holden (1875-1960), the imposing Art Deco Senate House (Grade II* listed) in Bloomsbury was constructed between 1933 and 1936. The building has 19 floors and is 210ft (64m) high, and when completed was the tallest secular building in Britain, constructed of the finest materials available, including

Portland stone, Travertine marble, English walnut and South American cypress. It was also the first building in the UK to be heated by electricity.

Senate House is the administrative centre of the University of London – the university's first permanent home – and houses the unique resources of Senate House Library, one of the world's largest humanities' collections. Members of the public can enjoy paid access to the library.

University of London, Senate House, Malet St, WC1E 7HU (020-7862 8000; www.london.ac.uk/ aboutsenatehouse.html; Russell Sq tube).

The Shard

One of London's most iconic and striking buildings – and the tallest in Western Europe at 1,016ft (309.6m) – the Shard was conceived (on the back of a menu) by Italian architect and engineer Renzo Piano (b. 1937), and completed in 2012. Designed as a building with multiple uses, a vertical city where people could live, work and relax, the Shard comprises prestigious offices, award-winning restaurants, the 5-star Shangri-La Hotel, exclusive residences and the UK's highest viewing gallery on the 72nd floor (802ft).

Taking inspiration from the spires of London churches and the masts of tall ships depicted by the 18th-century Venetian painter Canaletto, Renzo Piano designed the Shard as a spire-like sculpture emerging from the River Thames. The building is a spectacular glass and steel spire (clad in 11,000 glass panels) extending to 95 storeys, tapering off and disappearing into the sky.

You can experience a 360-degree panorama of London from the Shard's viewing platform, but it's best to avoid the astronomical fee and instead have lunch, afternoon tea or dinner at one of the Shard's many restaurants and bars (www. the-shard.com/restaurants). Not a cheap option, but at least the view's 'free'!

The Shard, 32 London Bridge St, SE1 9SG (www. the-shard.com; London Br tube; see www. theviewfromtheshard.com for viewing platform times and bookings).

Thames Barrier

The Thames Barrier was completed in 1982 and is one of the largest movable flood barriers in the world, extending 1,700ft (520m) across the River Thames and protecting 48mi^2 (125km$^{2)}$) of central London from flooding caused by tidal surges. It comprises ten steel gates, each weighing 3,700 tonnes which, when raised into position across the river, are over 65ft (20m) high and as wide as the opening of Tower Bridge.

The Thames Barrier Information Centre has an exhibition showing how the Barrier was built and how it works. There's no access onto the Barrier itself but there are riverside walkways with excellent views, a café and, on the north bank of the Thames, a park.

Thames Barrier, 1 Unity Way, SE18 5NJ (020-8305 4188; www.gov.uk/guidance/the-thames-barrier; Charlton or Woolwich Dockyard rail; visitor centre, Thu-Sun 10.30am-5pm, see website for prices).

Tower Bridge

Constructed between 1886 and 1894, Tower Bridge takes its name from the nearby Tower of London (see opposite) and is a combined bascule – a moveable bridge which 'opens' to allow ships to pass through – and suspension bridge. It's an iconic symbol of London and one of the most famous bridges in the world.

The Bridge houses an exhibition which uses films, photos and interactive displays to explain why and how the bridge was built, and visitors can also see the original lifting machinery in the Victorian engine rooms. The high-level walkways offer stunning views of the River Thames and London's landmarks, and incorporate a glass floor offering a unique if unnerving spectacle of the Bridge.

Tower Bridge, Tower Bridge Rd, SE1 2UP (020-7403 3761; www.towerbridge.org.uk; Tower Hill tube; see website for opening hours, tours and prices).

Tower of London

Palace, fortress, armoury, treasury and prison, the Tower of London has performed many roles since it was built in 1078 by William the Conqueror. Almost 1,000 years later the Tower remains an awesome sight, attracting some 2.5 visitors a year and is the UK's most popular historic attraction. The Tower refers to the White Tower, the keep at the heart of the castle, although it has become the catch-all name for the entire complex which includes over 20 towers.

A UNESCO World Heritage Site since 1988, the Tower is drenched in history, much of it of the dark and bloody variety. It's where Anne Boleyn and Katherine Howard were beheaded – a memorial marks the spot of the executioner's block on Tower Green – and where Edward IV's two young sons were allegedly murdered by Richard III.

For its first 500 years or so, it was a royal residence and centre of administration. Its notoriety as a place of imprisonment comes from Tudor times and later, and among the many well-known figures 'sent to the Tower' were Elizabeth I, Sir Walter Raleigh, Guy Fawkes and even East End gangsters Ronnie and Reggie Kray. Most escaped with their lives.

With such a colourful history – and the Crown Jewels on display – it's the perfect (although expensive!) place for a day out with the kids.

Tower of London, Tower Hill, EC3N 4AB (020-3166 6000; www.hrp.org.uk/toweroflondon; Tower Hill tube or riverboat to Tower Pier; see website for opening hours and prices).

3.

Cafés & Restaurants

It's hard to believe today, but London's restaurant scene was once the subject of international derision. The city has seen a gastronomic revolution in the last few decades and now offers some of the best and most varied dining anywhere. Indeed, London is one of the gourmet capitals of the world, ranked alongside Paris, New York and Hong Kong, with a vast choice of innovative eateries catering to all tastes and budgets.

Just as much as its inventive chefs and Michelin-starred restaurants, it's the city's incredible ethnic diversity that makes it such an exciting place to eat. In London, the world really is your oyster… it's also your bagel, bammy, chaat, dim sum, enchilada, falafel, injera, kimchi, lahmacun, pierogi, ravioli, satay or tapa! Introduced by immigrants, all are eagerly devoured by a population seeking gastronomic adventures.

London also has a flourishing independent café scene that has done much to cement its position as one of the world's leading foodie destinations. A far cry from the soggy sandwiches and stewed tea of yesteryear, today's café culture revolves around artisan coffee prepared by independent roasters, specialist teas from around the world, and a feast of delicious homemade food.

Price Guide: £ = inexpensive, ££ = moderate, £££ = expensive, ££££ = splurge

Barrica

If you love tapas then you'll be passionate about Barrica, an authentic Spanish eatery – awarded a Michelin Bib Gourmand in 2016-2017 – which wouldn't be out of place in Barcelona or Madrid. Whether you want a coffee and pastry, some olives, jamón or queso manchego with a glass of fino, or a full-blown Iberian feast with superb Spanish wines, Barrica fits the bill.

With its friendly atmosphere and reasonable prices, it's a great place for a snack, a leisurely lunch, or an evening lingering over tapas and sherry. *¡Salud!*

Barrica, 62 Goodge St, W1T 4NE (020-7436 9448; www.barrica.co.uk; Goodge St tube; Mon-Fri noon-11.30pm, Sat noon-11.30pm, closed Sun; Spanish tapas; ££).

Bistrotheque

Occupying a converted factory in an uninspiring East End location, Bistrotheque is a breath of fresh air, managing to be both elegant and contemporary at the same time, with sparkling white décor, high ceilings and industrial chic. The menu is more French-style than truly Gallic, offering the likes of mackerel pâté and steak tartare alongside cod and chips and cheeseburgers.

The *prix fixe* menu (available before 7pm) is good value at £20 for three courses and there's a popular weekend brunch too. Drop-ins can eat at the large oval bar (the Manchichi), which also serves divine cocktails.

Bistrotheque, 23-27 Wadeson St, E2 9DR (020-8983 7900; www.bistrotheque.com; Cambridge Heath rail; open daily – see website for times; modern French; ££).

Brasserie Zedel

Tuck into traditional French cuisine at buzzy Brasserie Zedel, a Parisian grand café, bar and brasserie from the prolific Chris Corbin and Jeremy King partnership. The vast subterranean dining room is a vision of La Belle Époque, with the ambience of an ocean liner during the golden era of transatlantic travel.

All the brasserie favourites are here, including classic onion soup, escargots, celeriac rémoulade, frisée with lardons, pâté de champagne, steak haché, boeuf bourguignon, duck confit, *choucroute*, tarte au citron, heavenly tarte tatin and much more.

Above all, Zedel is terrific value, offering a taste of the gastro palaces of Paris for the price of your local Café Rouge, including the bargain *prix fixe* at £9.75 for two courses (£12.75 for three) and the *formule* (£19.75 for three courses plus a glass of wine, water and coffee). The short wine list starts at around £16 a bottle, with almost everything below £30, while cocktails start from around £6.50. The restaurant is rated three stars by the Sustainable Restaurant Association (thesra.org), so you'll be helping save the planet. And if you want to make a night of it, there's also a glitzy cabaret and nightclub.

Brasserie Zedel, 20 Sherwood St, W1F 7ED (020-7734 4888; www.brasseriezedel.com; Piccadilly Circus tube; Mon-Sat 11.30am-midnight, Sun 11.30am-11pm; French; ££).

Caravan

You can eat your way around the world at Caravan, a cool, trendy café-restaurant, bar and coffee roastery in Farringdon's bustling Exmouth Market. With huge windows overlooking the market, the restaurant has an outdoorsy feel, which is enhanced during fine weather when the doors are folded back to allow alfresco dining. The room has a casual vibe and funky industrial design – wooden tables, white pipework and trendy light fittings – although the mouth-watering food is the star attraction.

There are three menus – breakfast (weekdays, 8-11.30am), brunch (weekends 10am-4pm) and an all-day lunch and dinner menu offering small and large sharing plates – employing seasonal ingredients to create inventive dishes featuring flavours from around the globe. The fashionable

term is fusion food, but this is like no fusion food you've ever tasted – in a good way!

Breakfast treats include banana caramel porridge, and smoked black pudding with roast apples and a fried egg, while the main menu includes miso-cured salmon with pickled daikon, red onion and *furikake* (Japanese seasoning), and slow-roasted rabbit with herb polenta, heritage carrots and golden raisins. It's innovative and unusual, but at Caravan unusual is the norm and the norm is fantastic!

There's also great coffee, plus interesting wines – all at reasonable prices.

Caravan, 11-13 Exmouth Mkt, EC1R 4QD (020-7833 8115; www.caravanrestaurants.co.uk/exmouth-market.html; Farringdon tube; see website for opening times; global; ££).

Chez Bruce

You can expect a magnificent meal at the Michelin-starred Chez Bruce, a restaurant with fine foodie credentials (in an earlier incarnation it was Harvey's, where Marco Pierre White, the enfant terrible of celebrity chefs, cut his teeth). It's one of London's very best places to eat and is consistently rated the city's favourite

restaurant by readers of Harden's *London Restaurants* guide.

The superb food is based loosely on classical and regional French/ Mediterranean cuisine. It may lack the histrionic flourishes, showmanship and theatricality that many restaurants indulge in nowadays, and some may view this as old-fashioned, but foodies and gourmets delight in the wonderful cooking, relaxed ambience, superb service and excellent value.

Chez Bruce, 2 Bellevue Rd, SW17 7EG (020-8672 0114; www.chezbruce.co.uk; Wandsworth Common rail; open daily – see website for times; French/Mediterranean; ££-£££).

Climpson & Sons

Climpson & Sons was founded by Ian Burgess, who was inspired by five years of drinking coffee in Australia to set up a stall in Hackney's Broadway Market. He moved into an old butcher's shop (from which his coffee emporium takes its name) and went on to become one of London's pioneer roasters, supplying many of the city's best coffee bars

Climpson's flagship café is a Mecca for coffee enthusiasts, offering a range of brew methods while exploring the best flavour profiles and extraction techniques. There's a comprehensive selection of beans for sale plus home-brewing equipment, so you can recreate some Climpson's magic at home.

Climpson & Sons, 67 Broadway Mkt, E8 4PH (020-7254 7199; www.climpsonandsons.com; London Fields rail; Mon-Fri 7.30am-5pm, Sat 8.30am-5pm, Sun 9am-5pm; £).

Counter Café

Established in 2009, the Counter Café is located in the Stour Space Gallery (www.stourspace.co.uk), a huge ramshackle community arts centre on an industrial estate in Hackney Wick. The location may not sound too attractive, but the independent café and coffee roastery offers panoramic views of the River Lee Navigation canal and the Olympic Stadium (just 100m away). It's a bright, laid-back

café occupying a large inviting space with the bonus of a fantastic outdoor terrace (pontoon) on the canal.

Run by siblings Tom and Jess from Auckland, the Counter Café does perfect coffee, delicious cakes and pastries, soups, salads, historic pies and an epic breakfast-brunch menu.

Counter Café, 7 Roach Rd, E3 2PA (07834-275920; http://counterproductive.co.uk; Hackney Wick rail; Mon-Fri 8am-5pm, Sat-Sun 9am-5pm: £).

The Dairy

Chef Robin Gill and his wife Sarah previously worked at Le Manoir aux Quat'Saisons, so it isn't surprising that The Dairy (bar and bistro) has received voluminous praise for its superb modern British cuisine and attention to detail.

The menu varies depending on the season and what's available in the restaurant's own urban garden (other produce is impeccably sourced), with daily specials for both lunch and dinner. The four-course lunch (served Wed-Fri) is a snip at £25. Don't let the venue's unremarkable (but cool) appearance fool you, this is seriously good cooking.

The Dairy, 15 The Pavement, SW4 0HY (020-7622 4165; http://the-dairy.co.uk; Clapham Common tube; see website for opening times; modern British; ££).

Federation Coffee

Buzzing Brixton Market is one of London's best eating and drinking destinations (and a great place to shop for food). It's also the home of Federation Coffee, Antipodean owned and operated and one of the best coffee shops in south London. Federation roast their own coffee using an ever-changing blend of coffees from Brazil, Ethiopia, El Salvador and Sumatra, and make all their own fresh food.

The vast menu includes over 100 sweet and savoury options – changing daily – all made in their own kitchen (also in the market). Try the super flat white or mocha accompanied by a cherry coconut slice or some moreish cheesecake.

People flock to this attractive café which is a good place to check your email or surf the web, chat with friends or simply hang out and watch the characters that frequent Brixton Village drift by. There are only around a dozen tables, so you may have to share, but the locals are a friendly bunch. Excellent service, relaxed neighbourhood atmosphere, and good coffee and food in one of London's most cosmopolitan areas.

Federation Coffee, Unit 77-78, Brixton Village, Coldharbour Ln, SW9 8PS (http://federationcoffee.com; Brixton tube; Mon-Fri 8am-5pm, Sat 9am-6pm, Sun 9am-5pm; £).

Fernandez & Wells

Fernandez & Wells started life in 2007 in Soho's Lexington Street and now boasts six outlets (see website), of which this is the largest and grandest. It occupies three impressive rooms in the east wing of 18th-century Somerset House, where Jorge Fernandez and Rick Wells have transported their signature Spanish 'street-style' café into a lovely light space with views over the courtyard and fountain. The décor incorporates York stone, wood and metal; oversized paintings by British artist David Tremlett decorate the walls, while a long cool bar bisects the main café area.

Spain dominates the menu, which revolves around coffee, cured meats, cheese and wine, and takes in breakfast, lunch and dinner. There's a wide choice of tasty tapas, inventive sandwiches (try the aubergine, goat's cheese and pesto in a brioche bun) and splendid soups such as classic gazpacho. The 'ham room', where plump hams hang from the wall, dispenses slices of lomito ibérico and jamón de lampiño – ham to die for!

There's also a range of enticing homemade cakes and pastries, including old-fashioned Eccles cakes. Excellent service and lip-smacking, value-for-money food. ¡Fantástico!

Fernandez & Wells, Somerset House, Strand, WC2R 1LA (020-7420 9408; www. fernandezandwells.com; Temple tube; Mon-Fri 8am-10pm, Sat 10am-10pm, Sun 10am-8pm; £).

Gokyuzu

A long-established, family-run restaurant, Gokyuzu's authentic eastern Mediterranean cuisine has been enthusing diners in this north London Turkish enclave for over 15 years. This superb – and under-rated – cuisine was conceived for the tables of the Ottoman Sultans and was once considered to be the most sophisticated fare in the world. The classic dishes are prepared in a traditional wood oven or on a charcoal grill using

authentic Mediterranean ingredients and spices – such as lamb, aubergines, cumin and mint – and include amazing mezze, wonderful kebabs and *pide* (Turkish pizza) to die for.

Huge portions and outstanding value for money; well worth queuing at busy times.

Gokyuzu, 26-27 Grand Parade, Green Lanes, N4 1LG (020-8211 8406; www.gokyuzurestaurant. co.uk; Harringay Green Lanes rail; daily 8am-1am; Turkish; ££).

Hakkasan Hanway Place

One of London's sexiest venues, Hakkasan Hanway Place is the original Hakkasan Chinese restaurant (there's another in Mayfair), which opened in 2001 and spawned a global empire. Its Michelin star was the first ever awarded to a Chinese restaurant, and deservedly so. The striking dining room (in black and gold) provides a dramatic background for Hakkasan's brand of glitzy Cantonese cuisine. Smouldering incense, seductive spot lighting and a gentle soundtrack help create a nightclub atmosphere, while the open-plan kitchen adds to the theatrical experience.

In addition to the à la carte menu there are themed 'Signature' and 'Taste of Hakkasan' menus and 'Dim Sum Sundays'. Cool, sexy, expensive – but unforgettable!

Hakkasan Hanway Place, 8 Hanway Pl, W1T 1HD (020-7927 7000; www. hakkasan.com/ hanwayplace; Tottenham Court Rd tube; see website for opening times; Chinese; £££-££££).

Honey & Co.

Honey & Co. is a delightful small café-restaurant and bakery in Fitzrovia specialising in food from the Middle East. Run by husband-and-wife team Itamar Srulovich and Sarit Packer, both of whom have worked at Ottolenghi (Sarit was also executive chef at NOPI) and know their *shakshouka* from their *muhamra*!

It's a tiny venue with a beautiful Moroccan-tiled floor, a clutch of tables and basic white-walled décor, but don't let the small space put you off. The food here is big and bold – a treat for the eyes and the taste buds – and also great value.

Honey & Co., 25A Warren St, W1T 5LZ (020-7388 6175; http://honeyandco.co.uk; Warren St tube; Mon-Fri 8am-10.30pm, Sat 9.30am-10.30pm, closed Sun; Middle Eastern; £-££).

Lantana Fitzrovia

The highly-rated, award-winning Lantana (an Australian flowering plant) opened in Fitzrovia in 2008, since when it has gone from strength to strength and spawned branches in Shoreditch and Camden. Lantana serves delicious coffee and is famous for its big Aussie-style breakfasts, lunches and weekend all-day brunches, not forgetting its excellent selection of baked goodies, which includes raspberry friands – a muffin-like cake – and cherry cake. It's licensed, too.

There's a cosy Antipodean atmosphere with wooden tables, mismatched chairs and art on the white walls, and seating both indoors and outside – although never quite enough – and it can get noisy at busy times.

Lantana Café, 13 Charlotte Pl, W1T 1SN (020-7637 3347; http://lantanacafe.co.uk; Goodge St tube; Mon-Fri 8am-6pm, Sat-Sun 9am-5pm; £).

Little Social

Across the street from his flagship restaurant, Pollen Street Social, Jason Atherton's Little Social follows the fashion for French bistros/brasseries which has seen such venues as Balthazar and Brasserie Zedel (see page 45) open in recent years. Designed in classic 'speakeasy style', the dining room has blood-red leather banquettes, faux-Lalique lampshades, vintage Michelin maps, a long bar lined with stools, plus neon for a dash of Manhattan chic.

With first-rate bold cooking, interesting wines, inspired cocktails, charming staff, an intimate atmosphere and affordable prices – in particular the *prix fixe* menu – Little Social is a winner all the way.

Little Social, 5 Pollen St, W1S 1NE (020-7870 3730; www.littlesocial.co.uk; Oxford Circus tube; Mon-Sat noon-2.30pm, 6-10.30pm, closed Sun; French; ££).

Look Mum No Hands!

One of the few places in London where you can have coffee and cake while getting your bike serviced, Look Mum No Hands! is a café/bar, bike repair shop and events venue catering to the cool new breed of London cyclists. The café occupies a vast space with plenty of tables, excellent coffee by Square Mile and filling food – you can also get a beer or a glass of wine.

A cyclist's Mecca, it shows cycle sports (e.g. Tour de France) on a huge projector screen and the workshop offers bicycle maintenance courses.

Look Mum No Hands!, 49 Old St, EC1V 9HX (020-7253 1025; www.lookmumnohands.com; Barbican or Old St tube/rail; Mon-Fri 7.30am-10pm, Sat 8.30am-10pm, Sun 9am-10pm: £).

Manuka Kitchen

Manuka Kitchen was founded by Kiwi chef Tyler Martin and wine expert Joseph Antippa (both formerly of the Gore Hotel). As you might expect, manuka honey features on the menu, although the name is more a nod to Martin's New Zealand roots. The stylish restaurant has high ceilings and large windows, while its rustic décor of terracotta tiles, white walls and simple wooden tables gives it a homely feel.

But it's the food that's the star here. Martin is a chef who's going places and his delicious, imaginative cuisine is a joy. Combined with its excellent wines, friendly service, great atmosphere and reasonable prices, it's almost perfect.

Manuka Kitchen, 510 Fulham Rd, SW6 5NJ (020-7736 7588; www.manukakitchen.com; Fulham Broadway tube; Mon 6-10pm, Tue-Thu noon-11pm, Fri-Sat 10am-11pm, Sun 10am-5pm; modern European; £-££).

The Modern Pantry

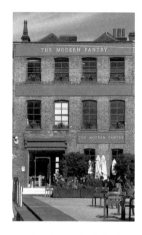

With a relaxed, calm setting and charming ambience, the Modern Pantry in Clerkenwell is noted for its flavoursome, imaginative food and formidable wines. Chef Anna Hansen's culinary philosophy is to excite the palate by fusing everyday ideas with unusual ingredients and global inspiration. Her food is a synthesis of east meets west: experimental, playful and touched with magic. Not everything works perfectly, but when it does – which is most of the time (like her strawberry, lemongrass & black sesame 'trifle') – the results are sublime.

There's also a separate café on the ground floor and a delicatessen next door (and another outlet in Finsbury Square).

The Modern Pantry, 47-48 St John's Sq, EC1V 4JJ (020-7553 9210; www.themodernpantry. co.uk; Farringdon tube; open daily – see website for times; fusion; ££).

Monmouth Coffee

One of the pioneers of the first wave of coffee shops and roasters that have been brewing up a storm in London, Monmouth opened their first roast-and-retail outlet in Covent Garden's Monmouth Street (hence the name) in 1978. Roasting is now done in Maltby Street (Bermondsey), from where they supply coffee shops throughout the city, and they also have an outlet in Borough Market.

The Covent Garden café is a simple affair by today's standards, with snug tables

in the back and a few benches outside. There's a tempting array of cakes and pastries – including lovely croissants and pain au chocolat – plus filled rolls and other goodies, but coffee is king here.

Monmouth Coffee, 27 Monmouth St, WC2H 9EU (020-7232 3010; www.monmouthcoffee.co.uk; Covent Gdn tube; Mon-Sat 8am-6.30pm, closed Sun: £).

Moro

Eat your way around the southern Mediterranean, courtesy of Moro in Exmouth Market, established in 1997 by 'the Sams' – Sam(uel) and Sam(antha) Clark. Moro offers a delectable fusion of Spanish, Middle Eastern and North African comfort food – such as garlicky boquerones with crusty bread and tender chargrilled squid coated in harissa – much of which is cooked in a wood-fired oven or char-grilled.

Moro's buzzy and sensual dining room is one of London's hottest tickets, so be prepared to book well in advance. You can also eat at the bar from the excellent tapas menu (all day, except for Sundays) and enjoy the excellent Iberian wine list. Heaven!

Moro, 34-36 Exmouth Mkt, EC1R 4QE (020-7833 8336; www.moro.co.uk; Farringdon tube; Mon-Sat 12.30-2.30pm, 6-10.30pm, Sun 12.30-2.45pm; Spanish/N African; ££).

The Nordic Bakery

Opened in 2007 by Finn Jali Wahlsten, this delightful Scandinavian-style café is a peaceful retreat; spacious and airy, minimalist but stylish, with a combination of wood-lined and deep blue walls. Golden Square is the original but there are two more Nordic Bakeries in W1.

The food is based on genuine Nordic recipes and ingredients and includes the house favourite cinnamon buns (and many other varieties of bun), plus delicious open sandwiches on rye bread with toppings including prawns, gravadlax, pickled herring, hard-boiled egg, brie and lingonberries. Cakes are scrumptious and the coffee is good and strong; if you want something different to drink, try the blueberry cordial. A Scandi star.

Nordic Bakery, 14A Golden Sq, W1F 9JG (020-3230 1077; www.nordicbakery.com; Piccadilly Circus tube; Mon-Fri 7.30am-8pm, Sat 8.30am-7pm, Sun 9am-7pm: £).

Ottolenghi

Yotam Ottolenghi's acclaimed eatery in Islington (opposite the Almeida Theatre) showcases his trademark Middle Eastern dishes: a beguiling marriage of explosive Mediterranean and Asian flavours in a palette of vibrant colours. It's one of the deli chain's few 'proper' café-restaurants, seating some 50 diners around communal tables in a cool, sophisticated environment.

Ottolenghi is open for breakfast, lunch and dinner, although bookings are only accepted at Upper Street for dinner, so if you fancy tucking into the legendary weekend brunch you need to arrive early. It's also a terrific place for vegetarians.

Yotam also has delis in Belgravia, Notting Hill and Spitalfields, a Soho-based restaurant, plus a wealth of cookbooks.

Ottolenghi, 287 Upper St, N1 2TZ (020-7288 1454; www.ottolenghi.co.uk; Highbury & Islington tube; Mon-Sat 8am-10.30pm, Sun 9am-7pm; Middle Eastern; ££).

Polpo Soho

Polpo (Italian for octopus) is an inspired restaurant in Soho modelled on a *bàcaro*, a humble Venetian restaurant serving simple food and young local wines. (Coincidentally, 41 Beak St was once home to the Venetian painter Canaletto.) It's the brainchild of co-owner Russell Norman, who toured Venice's back-street wine bars and *bàcari* in search of authentic flavours. The shabby-chic styling, however, is more New York Soho diner, with rough brick walls, tiled floors and scuffed plaster, brown-paper menus and glass tumblers.

Now part of a small chain, Polpo's award-winning, inventive take on Italian 'tapas' (*cicheti*) has spawned imitators across the capital. The great-value small plates include the likes of braised octopus (what else?) with Treviso lettuce and borlotti beans; spinach, parmesan and egg pizzette (mini pizza); sliced flank steak with rocket and parmesan; lamb and green peppercorn meatballs; and much more. Wines are

served in carafes (three sizes) and start from £6 for 250ml. Evening bookings are limited (walk-ins welcome), but you can book for lunch or grab a free bar seat.

Polpo has a great atmosphere, heavenly food, friendly service and is brilliant value. And if you want to take the experience home with you, there's a lovely cookbook containing 140 recipes from the restaurant.

Polpo Soho, 41 Beak St, W1F 9SB (020-7734 4479; www.polpo.co.uk; Oxford/Piccadilly Circus tube; Mon-Fri 11.30am-11pm, Sat 10am-11pm, Sun 10am-10pm; Italian; ££).

Prufrock Coffee

Prufrock's flagship café on buzzy Leather Lane is a shrine to coffee, founded by the legendary Gwilym Davies, a former UK and World Barista Champion (and no, he isn't from Down Under – he's a Yorkshireman). Davies is at the forefront of coffee's 'third wave': a movement to raise awareness of coffee as an artisan product, focusing as much on provenance as wine-making does.

Prufrock has its own in-house bakery and offers a seasonal menu using ingredients from many of London's best producers. The bright and bustling café is also home to the London Barista Resource and Training Centre, one of the city's leading coffee schools, and sells coffee beans and coffee-making equipment.

Prufrock Coffee, 23-25 Leather Ln, EC1N 7TE (020-7242 0467; www.prufrockcoffee.com; Farringdon tube; Mon-Fri 8am-6pm, Sat-Sun 10am-5pm; £).

The Riding House Café

The ultra-cool Riding House Café styles itself 'a modern all-day brasserie', offering breakfast, lunch, dinner, weekend brunch, Sunday lunch, and everything in between. There's even a separate bar with comprehensive cocktail and wine lists. The café has individual place settings or you can sit at the grand communal refectory table; there's also a secluded dining room and lounge, not forgetting the bar.

Famous for its delicious breakfasts, the brunch, lunch and dinner menus bring on a broad range of dishes, from tapas-style small plates to full-sized brasserie mains and (on Sundays!) a choice of Sunday roast – or you can just have a coffee and cake or a cocktail. Fabulous!

Riding House Café, 43-51 Great Titchfield St, W1W 7PQ (020-7927 0840; www.ridinghousecafe. co.uk; Oxford Circus tube; Mon-Thu 7.30am-11.30pm, Fri 7.30am-12.30am, Sat 8.30am-12.30am, Sun 9am-10.30pm; brasserie classics; ££).

The Table Café

The Table Café is one of Southwark's hidden gems, founded by Shaun Alpine-Crabtree and partners from the architectural practice Allies & Morrison. Occupying the ground floor of the architects' office, it consists of a large Scandinavian-style room with clean modern lines, floor-to-ceiling glass windows, communal oak tables and stools at the counter.

The café offers a modern menu that emphasises its commitment to provenance, sustainable sourcing and quality British ingredients. The Table dishes up breakfast, lunch and 'pop-up' evening dinners (see website), plus a fantastic weekend brunch that's good enough to lure foodies from nearby Borough Market. Tasty, value-for-money dining in SE1.

The Table Café, 83 Southwark St, SE1 0HX (020-7401 2760; http://thetablecafe.com; Southwark tube; Mon-Fri 7.30am-4.30pm, Sat-Sun 8.30am-4.30pm: £).

Tayyabs

Founded as a small café in Whitechapel in 1972, family-owned Tayyabs gradually swallowed up its neighbours (including a pub) and developed into the thriving business you see today. It serves the finest Pakistani Punjabi cuisine, from its famous mixed grill and fiery grilled lamb chops to more traditional dahls and *masala channa* (spicy chickpeas). There are exquisitely spiced lamb curries, plus north Indian staples such as tikkas, kebabs, onion bhajis and delicious naan bread.

Tayyabs is one of London's most popular curry restaurants and there are long queues at peak times, so booking is essential. No alcohol is served but you can BYO and they'll uncork it for free.

Tayyabs, 83-89 Fieldgate St, E1 1JU (020-7247 8521; http://tayyabs.co.uk; Aldgate East or Whitechapel tube; daily noon-11.30pm; Punjabi; £-££).

10 Greek Street

The small, unprepossessing 10 Greek Street is a buzzy, cramped gem of a neighbourhood restaurant in Soho, serving inventive modern European cuisine. The short daily-changing menu is chalked up on a blackboard and includes the likes of pork and pistachio ballotine; wood pigeon with cauliflower, pine nuts and raisins; Brecon lamb, olive oil mash, kale and salsa verde; plaice with mussels, clams, monk's beard and baby leeks; and rum and caramel panna cotta with prunes. It's all delicious, good-value food. The impressive wine list was voted 'Great Value Wine List of the Year 2014' by *Imbibe* magazine.

Bookings taken for lunch (Mon-Sat, noon-2.30pm) but sadly there's a 'no reservations' policy for dinner (Mon-Sat, from 5.30pm).

10 Greek Street, W1D 4DH (020-7734 4677; www.10greekstreet.com; Tottenham Ct Rd tube; Mon-Sat noon-11pm, closed Sun; modern European; ££).

Trinity

Award-winning Trinity (three AA rosettes and a Michelin star) opened in 2006 and quickly put Clapham on the foodie map. Chef Adam Byatt's creative, flavoursome and beautifully-presented cuisine is a delight, with changing seasonal menus including a tasting menu, set lunch (good value) and Sunday lunch, which may include the likes of crab bisque, samphire and brown crab toastie; 40-day aged Dexter beef, Yorkshire pudding, horseradish, bone marrow and cauliflower cheese; and passion fruit and chocolate Eton mess. Scrummy!

The wine list runs to some 350 bins and wine lovers can expand their knowledge by attending one of the regular wine dinners in the upstairs dining space.

Trinity, 4 The Polygon, SW4 0JG (020-7622 1199; www.trinityrestaurant.co.uk; Clapham Common tube; Mon-Sat 12.30-2.30pm, 6.30-10pm, Sun 12.30-2.30pm, 7-9pm; modern British; ££-£££).

Workshop Coffee

This highly regarded coffee roaster opened its first café on Clerkenwell Road in 2011 (there are now four branches) and has been scooping up awards ever since, including 'Best Independent Café' at the 2012 Café Society Awards. Since then it has evolved into a thriving destination not only for coffee lovers but also for foodies, adding breakfast, lunch and weekend brunch to its repertoire. The décor is contemporary industrial chic, light and spacious with high ceilings, bare floorboards and exposed brick and pipes.

Scrumptious food and coffee, friendly service and a super atmosphere.

Workshop Coffee, 27 Clerkenwell Rd, EC1M 5RN (020-7253 5754; https://workshopcoffee. com; Farringdon tube; Mon 7.30am-6pm, Tue-Fri 7.30am-7pm, Sat-Sun 8am-6pm: £).

Zuma

Appropriately located in fashionable Knightsbridge, trendsetting Zuma offers a sophisticated take on the traditional Japanese *izakaya* (pub) style of informal eating and drinking, where food is usually ordered slowly over several courses with many dishes designed to be shared. It opened in 2002 but the

striking postmodern design – a mixture of steel, glass, wood, stone and granite – is still achingly trendy.

The authentic menu is comprehensive and alluring – packed with bold, intense flavours and showcasing fashionable ingredients such as Wagyu beef, langoustines, black cod, scallops and king crab. Even the desserts are fantastic; try the yuzu cheesecake with raspberry and black sesame.

Zuma, 5 Raphael St, SW7 1DL (020-7584 1010; www.zumarestaurant.com/zuma-landing/london/ en/restaurant; Knightsbridge tube; Mon-Fri noon-3pm, 6-11pm, Sat-Sun noon-3.30pm, 6-11pm, Sun until 10.30pm; Japanese; £££-££££).

4.

Cinemas & Theatres

No other city offers the breadth, variety and quality of theatre, cinema and dance as London, which boasts the largest theatre audience of any city in the world. Indeed, the history of London has been inextricably linked to that of the theatre for over 400 years since Shakespeare opened his Globe theatre on Bankside in 1599, and cinema for over 120 years. Today it boasts everything from traditional music halls to state-of-the-art IMAX cinemas, 18th-century West End theatres to intimate arthouse cinemas, 30-seater pub venues to Europe's largest arts centre.

For centuries locals and visitors have flocked to the burgeoning capital's West End – the world's largest theatre district – to be entertained and enchanted by world-class shows such as *The Mousetrap* and *Les Miserables*. With such a broad range of venues there's a continuous programme of premières, fringe productions, hit musicals, and vibrant modern and traditional dance.

Leicester Square is both the heart of Theatreland and the hub for cinema in the capital, with the red carpet being rolled out regularly for premieres at the Empire and Odeon theatres. Londoners love the cinema, and despite the advance of the multiplex the city is still home to many iconic picture houses, with gilded mouldings, plush velvet seats and stunning Art Deco interiors; just the place for a choc ice and matinee.

The Adelphi Theatre

Although it celebrated its bicentenary in 2006, the Adelphi Theatre (Grade II listed) on the Strand is the fourth on this site, which have operated under no fewer than seven different names. The current Art Deco theatre opened in 1930 under the name Royal Adelphi (the Royal epithet was

dropped in 1940). The front-of-house areas of the theatre were restored to their original splendour in 1993, when Andrew Lloyd Webber became the co-owner and opened his musical production of *Sunset Boulevard*.

In November 1997, the London production of the popular American musical *Chicago* premièred at the Adelphi and ran for eight and a half years, making it the longest-running American musical in West End history.

The Adelphi Theatre, Strand, WC2R 0NS (020-3725 7060; www.reallyusefultheatres.co.uk/our-theatres/adelphi; Charing Cross tube/rail).

The Almeida Theatre

Although its foundations date back to 1837, when it began life as a literary and scientific society (complete with library, lecture theatre and laboratory), the current Almeida Theatre opened in 1980 combining the best of its 19th-century original features with modern facilities. It's an intimate 325-seat studio theatre (dubbed a 'a small stage where giants play') with an international reputation, which takes its name from the street on which it's located, off Upper Street in Islington.

Extensively refurbished in 2001-03, the delightful Almeida is a launchpad for the next generation of British artists onto the world stage, producing an exciting programme of drama and plays, many of which transfer to West End theatres.

Almeida Theatre, Almeida St, N1 1TA (020-7359 4404; www.almeida.co.uk; Essex Rd rail/Angel tube).

The Barbican Arts Centre

A prominent example of British Brutalist concrete architecture and Europe's largest arts and conference venue, the Barbican Arts Centre (Grade II listed) stages a comprehensive range of art, music, theatre, dance, film and creative learning events. The centre hosts classical and contemporary music concerts, theatre performances, film screenings and art exhibitions. It's owned, funded, and

managed by the City of London Corporation, the third-largest funder of arts in the UK; and was built as the City's gift to the nation at a cost of £161 million and opened in 1982.

The centre comprises the 1,949-seat Barbican Hall, the 1,166-seat Barbican Theatre, the 200-seat Pit theatre, a 286-seat cinema, the Barbican Art Gallery, 'The Curve' gallery, plus a library, lakeside terrace, conservatory, gardens and three restaurants. It's home to the London Symphony Orchestra and the BBC Symphony Orchestra is also based in the Barbican Centre's concert hall.

The Centre's theatres offer everything from gritty reality to far-flung fantasy, from dance to drama, from established artists to those just beginning their careers. It was the London base of the Royal Shakespeare Company for many years, but has since moved on from traditional British to experimental international theatre, and is packed with exciting, unexpected and intriguing offerings, incorporating everything from cabaret to classical.

The Barbican Arts Centre, Silk St, EC2Y 8DS (020-7638 4141; www.barbican.org.uk; Barbican tube).

BFI IMAX

The amazing BFI IMAX cinema (not to be confused with BFI Southbank, a four-screen art cinema) is located in a futuristic seven-storey, glass-enclosed cylinder situated in the centre of a busy roundabout next to Waterloo station. With its vast 26m x 20m (520m^2) screen – the largest in the UK – 12,000w digital, surround-sound system and stunning IMAX technology,

the 500-seat BFI IMAX is the most technically impressive cinema in the country. There's also no chance of a head blocking your view as the seats are positioned at a vertiginous angle. Watching a film here is a completely immersive experience, ranging from the latest IMAX blockbusters to world-class alternative content and educational presentations. Not cheap but well worth the premium.

BFI IMAX, 1 Charlie Chaplin Walk, South Bank, SE1 8XR (0330-333 7878; www.bfi.org.uk/bfi-imax; Southwark tube).

Curzon Cinema Mayfair

Part of a small chain, the Curzon Cinema Mayfair (Grade II listed) is one of London's oldest (1934) and most prestigious art-house cinemas, with two screens and a stylish bar. The largest of its two plush auditoriums – all blue carpeted floors and velvet armchairs – has 311 seats and two original royal boxes (which can be hired), while the smaller screen is a snug 83-seater.

The programme is a mix of art-house films, live events and documentaries. It was one of the first cinemas to import and show foreign language films in the UK, and nowadays also screens live performances, including satellite transmissions from the National Theatre, London's Royal Opera House and the Metropolitan Opera in New York.

Curzon Cinema Mayfair, 38 Curzon St, W1J 7TY (0330-500 1331; www.curzoncinemas.com; Green Pk tube).

Donmar Warehouse Theatre

The Donmar Warehouse is a pioneering not-for-profit 251-seat theatre located in the heart of Covent Garden. Over the past 25 years it has built an enviable reputation for artistic excellence as one of the UK's leading producing theatres; working with theatre's finest creative artists, it has won over 100 major awards.

The theatre has presented some of the city's most memorable productions, showcased the talent of many of the industry's greats, including Kenneth Branagh and Sir Ian McKellen, and built up a superb body of work. The Donmar's diverse artistic policy encompasses bold re-imaginings of Shakespearean classics and innovative revivals of contemporary British, Irish and American drama, and is committed to bringing new plays to the stage.

Formed in the '60s in a former banana-ripening depot and owned for a while by the Royal Shakespeare Company, the Donmar was acquired in 1990 by Roger Wingate who rebuilt and re-equipped it, appointing Sam Mendes as its first artistic director. Since re-opening in 1992, Donmar productions have earned 45 Laurence Olivier Awards, 26 Critics' Circle Awards and 27 Evening Standard Awards, two South Bank Awards, as well as 20 Tony Awards for ten Broadway productions (and counting…).

Donmar Warehouse Theatre, 41 Earlham St, WC2H 9LX (0844-871 7624; www.donmarwarehouse.com; Covent Gdn tube).

Electric Cinema

London's first purpose-built cinema, the elegant Electric on Portobello Road (Grade II* listed) is one of the city's most romantic picture houses. It first opened in 1910 and since then has been renamed (in the '30s) and re-launched (in the '60s), while in the '40s (it's said) the Electric employed a notorious mass murderer in the projectionist's booth (John Christie of nearby 10 Rillington Place). In the '90s it was purchased by architects Gebler Tooth, who restored and upgraded the building with a restaurant, bar and private members' club, while retaining the glamour and elegance of the '30s.

Cinema goers relax in luxurious leather armchairs, with footstools and side tables offering unparalleled comfort. There are even a number of two-seater sofas at the rear and six decadent velvet-lined double beds (!) in the front row, providing a unique cinematic experience; cashmere blankets and a waiter delivering cocktails to your seat complete this cinematic heaven. The films aren't bad either and include both mainstream and art-house films.

If you want to make a night of it, pop into the Electric Diner next door for a shaved rib of beef sandwich or honey-fried chicken with chilli and sesame, washed down with a cool Nevada Pale Ale. And don't forget to try the Electric's sister cinema in Shoreditch, complete with its own barber shop!

Electric Cinema, 191 Portobello Rd, W11 2ED (020-7908 9696; www.electriccinema.co.uk; Ladbroke Grove tube).

Empire Leicester Square

One of London's oldest cinemas, the Empire Leicester Square opened in 1884 as the Empire Theatre, becoming a cinema in the '20s (when it showed silent films). After the Second World War the theatre was increasingly refurbished to enlarge the auditorium and uprate the equipment. The last redevelopment was in 2013, when the vast auditorium was split into one full IMAX screen – the largest IMAX in the UK by seating capacity (727) with the widest (curved) screen

at 26.5m x 15.6m – plus a second 400-seat theatre and seven smaller screens.

As you'd expect from a central London multiplex, the Empire screens all the latest blockbusters and is a popular venue for film premières.

Empire Leicester Square, 5-6 Leicester St, WC2H 7NA (0871-471 4714; www.cineworld.co.uk/cinemas/london-leicester-square; Leicester Sq tube).

Hackney Empire

Built in 1901, the Hackney Empire (Grade II* listed), with its electric lights, central heating and in-built projection box, was a technological wonder of its time, designed by the great Frank Matcham, one of Britain's most inventive theatre architects. Owned by Sir Oswald Stoll it attracted acts from all over the world, including Charlie Chaplin (who appeared a number of times before decamping to America), Stan Laurel and Marie Lloyd (the 'Queen of the Halls').

After an ignominious period as a bingo hall in the '60s and '70s, the renovated and modernised old dame still has them rolling in the aisles after 115 years, presenting a mixture of variety, comedy, drama, dance, opera and pantomime.

Hackney Empire, 291 Mare St, E8 1EJ (020-8985 2424; www.hackneyempire.co.uk; Hackney Central rail).

London Coliseum

Located in St Martin's Lane, the London Coliseum is one of the largest and most famous family variety theatres in London. Designed by Frank Matcham and opened in 1904, it was one of the city's finest music halls. It was used for a range of events including film screenings, musical comedies, plays and variety shows until, in 1968, the Sadler's Wells Opera Company (now the English National Opera) took it over.

With over 2,500 seats, the Coliseum is the largest theatre in London; it underwent extensive renovations in 2000-04, when a staircase originally planned (but not completed) was installed. Today, the splendour of the building is only matched by the superb performances of the English National Opera.

London Coliseum, St Martin's Ln, WC2N 4ES (020-7845 9300; www.eno.org; Leicester Sq tube).

Menier Chocolate Factory Theatre

One of the more unusual settings for a theatre, the Menier Chocolate Factory Theatre is located in a... renovated Victorian chocolate factory! The award-winning 150-seat theatre on London's South Bank opened in 2004, and the original exposed wooden beams, cast iron columns and brick interior of the 1870 factory building create a stimulating environment in which to enjoy a high-quality and entertaining theatrical experience.

The Menier is one of London's most dynamic fringe venues, presenting a mixture of musicals and light-hearted plays, with the occasional stand-up comedy or revue show imported from New York. There's also a chic restaurant and bar.

Menier Chocolate Factory Theatre, 53 Southwark St, SE1 1RU (020-7378 1713; www. menierchocolatefactory.com; London Bridge tube).

National Theatre

Widely considered to be one of the greatest theatres in the world, the (Royal) National Theatre (NT) is also one of London's most iconic landmarks and possibly the UK's foremost example of Brutalist architecture. Designed by Sir Denys Lasdun and opened in 1976, the NT boasts four auditoriums – the Olivier (1,160 seats), Lyttelton (890), Dorfman (400) and Temporary (225) – and its NT Live programme beams its performances to cinemas across the globe. The NT offers a mix of re-imagined classics, modern masterpieces, popular new writing and the odd experimental work.

The complex has a variety of eating and drinking facilities, including its flagship House Restaurant and the Understudy riverside bar, which brews its own lager and offers great music.

National Theatre, Upper Ground, SE1 9PX (020-7452 3000; www.nationaltheatre.org.uk; Waterloo tube/rail).

Odeon Leicester Square

Overlooking the eastern side of Leicester Square, the Art Deco flagship Odeon cinema dominates the square with its huge black polished granite façade and 120ft (37m) tower displaying its name. It's London's number one destination for red carpet (European and world) premières and the city's largest cinema with 1,683 seats. Opened in 1937, the Odeon retains its fully-operational (Compton) pipe organ and much of its striking (restored) '30s Art Deco interior decoration.

It's the largest single-screen cinema in the UK – and one of the few with its original circle and stalls intact – showing blockbusters in 2D and 3D formats.

Odeon Leicester Square, 24-26 Leicester Sq, WC2H 7JY (0333-014 4501; www.odeon.co.uk/cinemas/london_leicester_square/105; Leicester Sq tube).

Old Vic Theatre

Founded in 1818 as the Royal Coburg Theatre, the Old Vic (Grade II* listed) in southeast London was renamed the Royal Victoria Theatre in 1833 and the Royal Victoria Hall in 1880, by which time it was already dubbed the 'Old Vic'.

The Old Vic has had a greater influence on the history of drama than any theatre standing today and was the first to perform the complete works of William Shakespeare as a series. Long known as 'the actors' theatre' – Laurence Olivier claimed it had 'the most powerful actor/audience relationship in the world' – the Vic has played host to generations of stars, from John Gielgud and Laurence Olivier to Kevin Spacey and Judi Dench.

Old Vic Theatre, 103 The Cut, SE1 8NB (0844-871 7628; www.oldvictheatre.com; Waterloo tube/ rail).

Palace Theatre

An imposing red-brick structure dating from 1891, the Palace Theatre was designed by Thomas Edward Collcutt and commissioned by Richard D'Oyly Carte, who wanted the theatre to become the home of English grand opera. It opened as the Royal English Opera House, but has been the Palace Theatre since 1911 and the home of many popular musicals.

The later part of the 20th century saw two very successful runs at the Palace: *Jesus Christ Superstar*, which ran from 1972 until 1980, and *Les Misérables*, which opened in 1985 and ran for 19 years (7,602 performances) before transferring to The Queen's Theatre in 2004, where it remains today as the world's longest-running musical of all time.

Palace Theatre, Shaftesbury Ave, W1D 5AY (0844-412 4656; www.palacetheatrelondon.org; Leicester Sq tube).

Prince Charles Cinema

An independent cinema off Leicester Square, the Prince Charles offers a varied programme including cult, art house, quirky and classic films, alongside recent Hollywood blockbuster releases. There are also all-night sessions, double bills, short seasons, and special events such as 007 retrospectives and Sundays dedicated to Academy Award-winning Studio Ghibli (the Tokyo-based animation film studio).

Don't miss the sing-a-long-a nights, where audience participation is strongly encouraged and you can belt out your favourites from *The Sound of Music*, *Grease* or the *Rocky Horror Picture Show*. It isn't luxurious but it's super value (cheap as chips) and the programme is fantastic. Great fun!

Prince Charles Cinema, 7 Leicester Place, WC2H 7BX (020-7494 3654; www.princecharlescinema. com; Leicester Sq tube).

Prince of Wales Theatre

The Prince of Wales Theatre was designed by architect Charles J. Phipps and opened in 1884; it was subsequently rebuilt in 1937 to an Art Deco design by Robert Cromie and extensively refurbished in 2004 by current owner Sir Cameron Mackintosh, with seating for 1,140. Externally, the Grade II listed theatre looks modern, but the interior takes audiences back to the '20s and '30s, the golden age of theatre design.

Following the 2004 refurbishment, the theatre was reopened by HRH The Prince of Wales with a charity gala performance of *Mamma Mia!* This went on to become the theatre's longest-running show and in 2012 celebrated the 13th anniversary of its original London opening.

Prince of Wales Theatre, Coventry St, W1D 6AS (0844-482 5115; www.princeofwalestheatre. co.uk; Piccadilly Circus tube).

Royal Court Theatre

The Royal Court Theatre (Grade II listed) is a splendid Victorian-era playhouse that's the de facto home of modern English theatre. The current theatre was designed by Walter Emden and Bertie Crewe and opened in 1888 (as the New Court Theatre), built of fine red brick with a stone façade in free Italianate style. It had a chequered life for the first 70 years of its existence, serving variously as a receiving house (hosting touring companies), a producing venue and a cinema, before falling into disuse after bomb damage during the Second World War.

After the war the interior was reconstructed by Robert Cromie and the theatre re-opened in 1952. George Devine became artistic director and in 1956 his English Stage Company – Britain's first national subsidised theatre company – set up home at the Royal Court and began producing radical new work. Devine set out to discover new writers and produce serious contemporary works – his company's third production, in 1956, was John Osborne's *Look Back in Anger*, later seen as the starting point of modern British drama. Two decades later, in 1973, the *Rocky Horror Show* premièred at the Royal Court.

In the '90s the theatre was completely rebuilt, reopening in 2000, with the 370-seat proscenium-arch Jerwood Theatre Downstairs and the 85-seat Jerwood Theatre Upstairs. The Royal Court is an inspiration to writers, actors and audiences alike, and is worthy of any theatre lover's support.

Royal Court Theatre, Sloane Sq, SW1W 8AS (020-7565 5000; www.royalcourttheatre.com; Sloane Sq tube).

Royal Opera House

Also known simply as 'Covent Garden', this London icon has a long and fascinating history. The current building is the third to stand here – its predecessors, built in 1732 and 1808, were lost to fire – and was designed by Edward Middleton Barry. It dates from 1858, although only the façade, foyer and auditorium (Grade I listed) are original, following extensive reconstruction (costing £178 million) in the '90s. Today the ROH is home to the Royal Opera, the Royal Ballet and the Orchestra of the Royal Opera House.

The Royal Opera, under the direction of Antonio Pappano, is one of the world's leading opera companies, renowned for its outstanding performances of traditional opera and for commissioning new works. Many of the world's most famous singers have performed with the company, including Plácido Domingo, José Carreras, Renée Fleming, Juan Diego Flórez and Bryn Terfel, as well as the late Luciano Pavarotti and Joan Sutherland.

The Royal Ballet owes its existence to the vision of Dame Ninette de Valois – dancer, choreographer and entrepreneur – who assembled a small company and school, the Vic-Wells Ballet and, in 1931, persuaded Lilian Baylis to provide it with a home at the Sadler's Wells Theatre (see page 76). In 1946 they transferred to the Royal Opera House and in 1956, to mark the company's 25th anniversary, the name 'The Royal Ballet' was granted by Royal Charter. Today it's one the leading ballet companies in the world.

Royal Opera House, Bow St, WC2E 9DD (020-7304 4000; www.roh.org.uk; Covent Gdn tube).

Sadler's Wells Theatre

The nucleus of British contemporary dance, Sadler's Wells is the sixth theatre on this Clerkenwell site since its inception in 1683, when Richard Sadler built a music house around a mineral spring. The current theatre opened in 1998 and consists

of two performance spaces: the 1,500-seat main auditorium and the 180-seat Lilian Baylis Studio (it also leases the Peacock Theatre). It's dedicated to producing, commissioning and presenting the best of international and UK dance, and crossing the boundaries between different art forms. Sadler's Wells is a world leader in contemporary dance presenting a vibrant programme – from tango to hip-hop, ballet to Bollywood – showcasing the best of international and British dance.

Sadler's Wells Theatre, Rosebery Ave, EC1R 4TN (020-7863 8000; www.sadlerswells.com; Angel tube).

The Savoy Theatre

Opened in 1881 on the site of the old Savoy Palace in London, the Savoy Theatre (now Grade II listed) was the brainchild of Richard D'Oyly Carte who envisaged it as a showcase for the works of Gilbert and Sullivan. The Savoy Hotel, adjacent to the theatre and built in 1889, was funded from the profits of D'Oyley Carte's 'Savoy Operas'.

The first public building in the world to be lit entirely by electricity, the Savoy Theatre was restored in 1929 with a classic Art Deco foyer, and again in the early '90s following a fire. It has hosted the premieres of some world-famous works, from *The Mikado* to Noël Coward's *Blithe Spirit*, and its name is synonymous with quality drama, opera and musicals.

Savoy Theatre, Savoy Court, Strand, WC2R 0ET (0844-871 7687; www.savoytheatre.org and www.atgtickets.com/venues/savoy-theatre; Embankment/Temple tube).

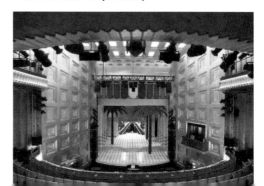

Shakespeare's Globe Theatre

The Globe can trace its heritage back to 1599 when its first incarnation was built by William Shakespeare's company, the Lord Chamberlain's Men. It was destroyed by fire in 1613 and a second Globe was erected in its place the following June; this continued until 1642 when the Puritans closed it down.

Today's modern reconstruction opened in 1997 on Bankside, approximately 750ft (230m) from the site of the original theatre. It's the only building in London permitted to have a thatched roof (due to fire regulations) and is faithful to the 1599 original in its design, using building techniques from 400 years ago. Although it isn't an exact replica, plays are performed in the open air, rain or shine, just as they were in the 17th century.

Founded by the pioneering American actor and director Sam Wanamaker (1919-1993), Shakespeare's Globe is dedicated to the exploration of the Bard's work and the playhouse for which he wrote. The design of the stage – jutting out into the auditorium – and the fact that cheap standing tickets are available for every performance create a raucous relationship between actors and audience that makes it unlike any other theatre. If you're standing, dress for the elements as there's no shelter.

In 2013, an indoor candlelit Jacobean theatre, the 340-seat Sam Wanamaker Theatre, was opened adjacent to the Globe to allow plays to take place year round.

Shakespeare's Globe Theatre, 21 New Globe Walk, SE1 9DT (020-7902 1400; www.shakespearesglobe.com; Southwark tube).

The Soho Theatre

A happy hunting ground for lovers of new theatre, comedy and cabaret, the Soho Theatre is both a theatre and a writers' development organisation (registered charity) of national significance. The theatre has three performance spaces: the 150-seat Soho Theatre, the 90-seat Soho Upstairs and a subterranean cabaret venue, Soho Downstairs. Together they stage at least four shows a night – booking isn't always necessary for the more intimate cabaret shows.

With a programme spanning theatre, comedy, cabaret and writers' events, and home to a lively bar, the Soho Theatre is one of the most vibrant venues on London's cultural scene.

Soho Theatre, 21 Dean St, W1D 3NE (020-7478 0100; www.sohotheatre.com; Tottenham Court Rd tube).

Theatre Royal Drury Lane

The Theatre Royal Drury Lane (Grade I listed) is one of London's oldest and most spectacular theatres. Designed by Benjamin Wyatt and opened in 1812, it's the most recent of four theatres built at the same location dating back to 1663. Its stage has been graced by actors as diverse as Shakespearean Edmund Kean, child actress Clara Fisher, comedian Dan Leno, playwright/actor Noël Coward and the comedy troupe Monty Python. Other claims to fame are that both the National Anthem and *Rule Britannia* were first performed here.

Today, the Theatre Royal stages mostly popular musical theatre and is owned by composer Andrew Lloyd Webber's Really Useful Group.

Theatre Royal Drury Lane, Catherine St, WC2B 5JF (0844-412 4660; www.reallyusefultheatres. co.uk/our-theatres/theatre-royal; Covent Gdn tube).

Theatre Royal Haymarket

The Theatre Royal, Haymarket (also known as the Haymarket Theatre or the Little Theatre in the Hay) is one of London's most famous theatres, originally designed and built by John Potter in 1720, making it the third-oldest London playhouse still in use. The original building was a little further north in the same street, but has been located at its current site since 1821, when it was redesigned by John Nash.

The Grade I listed theatre has had a colourful history, complete with riots, falling chandeliers and censorship, as well as plenty of smash hits. It was one of the city's most progressive theatres and in 1873 became the first to introduce a matinée performance. Plays and light comedies have generally characterised its programmes, with Oscar Wilde presenting many of his literary works here, including the premières of both *A Woman of No Importance* and *An Ideal Husband* in the 1890s.

Popular plays throughout the early 1900s included J. M. Barrie's *Mary Rose* (1920), Noël Coward's *Design for Living* (1939) and John Gielgud's early '40s season. The latter half of the 20th century saw works from writers such as Harold Pinter, Tennessee Williams, Terrence Rattigan, George Bernard Shaw and Tom Stoppard. The Haymarket still plays host to major stars in important productions, including in recent years *The Royal Family* starring Judi Dench and Terrence Rattigan's *Flare Path* starring Sienna Miller and Sheridan Smith.

Theatre Royal Haymarket, 18 Suffolk St, SW1Y 4HT (020-7930 8800; www.trh.co.uk; Piccadilly tube).

5.

Clubs

Londoon is home to numerous private members' clubs, many of which are among the most exclusive in the world, catering to captains of industry, media types, art lovers and even families. So whether you're seeking a social club, women's club, business club or something more conceptual, there are plenty to choose from, each with a different philosophy, membership and ambience

Many private clubs were set up to oil the wheels of their members' business dealings – most have meeting rooms and office equipment for members' use – but they're just as much about networking over a gin and tonic or an aromatherapy session. The best clubs offer sumptuous interiors, superb art collections, expertly mixed drinks, Michelin-standard food, gyms and spa facilities and – not least – a host of like-minded people to socialise with.

The drawback is that to rub shoulders with London's movers and shakers, you first have to get through the door; the most exclusive clubs levy high annual fees and have restrictive membership rules. Moreover, membership isn't simply a case of money: you may also need influential contacts, witty conversation and good manners! But if your application is rejected you can always take solace from Groucho Marx's famous quote: "I wouldn't want to belong to any club that would have me as a member."

12 Hay Hill

Although primarily a business club, 12 Hay Hill in Mayfair happily mixes business with pleasure: alongside fully-serviced offices with hot-desking, meeting/board rooms and business lounges, there's a Michelin-starred restaurant, lounge bar, café, exercise room, cigar terrace and humidor, and a concierge service. Dining options include a high-end brasserie with a menu based on Jersey chef Shaun Rankin's signature ingredients (e.g. scallops, crab and Jersey Royals), deli-style daytime dining in the basement bar, and a light menu for alfresco dining on the garden terrace overlooking Berkeley Square.

HH also features changing displays of contemporary art (for sale) from established names alongside promising new talent, a broad range of business, cultural and gastronomic events, and seminars with high quality speakers.

12 Hay Hill, W1J 6DQ (020-7952 6000; www.12hayhill.com; Green Pk tube; Mon-Thu 7am-11.30pm, Fri 7.30-1am, closed weekends).

The Arts Club

Founded in 1863 in the heart of bustling Mayfair, the exclusive Arts Club has been a haven for artists and patrons of the arts, literature and science (including art, architecture, fashion, film, literature, music, performance, photography, science, theatre and TV/media) for over 150 years. Featuring a salon, three restaurants, drawing room, bar and

conservatory, plus 16 luxury bedrooms and suites for members and their guests, it's an ideal spot for celeb-spotting – current members include Gwyneth Paltrow, Beyoncé and Ronnie Wood.

The club offers a comprehensive programme of events including poetry readings, cabaret performances and curated tours of arts institutions, in addition to staging revolving exhibitions of new and established artists.

The Arts Club, 40 Dover St, W1S 4NP (020-7499 8581; www.theartsclub.co.uk; Green Pk tube; Mon-Tue 7.30-1am, Wed-Fri 7.30-3am, Sat 8-3am, Sun 8am-midnight).

Blacks Club

Located in a beautifully restored 18th-century Georgian building in Soho, Blacks Club is a bohemian private members' club founded by Tom Bantock (a famous Norfolk poacher) in 1992. However, the club can trace its origins back to 1764, when Samuel Johnson, David Garrick and Joshua Reynolds formed a supper club here. Today, Blacks remains true to its supper-club roots with fine food and an extensive drinks list (signature cocktails are inspired by the club's Hogarth prints).

It's the perfect hideaway for arts and media eccentrics who enjoy witty, stimulating conversation: the criteria for applying for membership is that you are extraordinarily interesting and interested! It also welcomes dogs.

Blacks Club, 67 Dean St, W1D 4QH (020-7287 3381; www.blacksclub.com; Leicester Sq tube; Mon-Fri 10-1am, Sat 5pm-1am, closed Sundays).

Broadway House

The brainchild of club guru Brenhan Magee, Broadway House boasts a restaurant, grill, library, lounge, champagne/cocktail bar, private meeting rooms, an outdoor cinema and two stunning roof terraces. It's a unique haven of style and is a regular backdrop for C4's reality TV series *Made in Chelsea*.

The Broadway compromises four floors (5,000ft^2) of dining and drinking experiences: the Broadway Bar and Grill on the ground floor, the Brasa Restaurant on the first floor – both open to the public – plus the Broadway Private Members' Club and terrace on the second floor, and a rooftop bar (which is covered in winter).

Broadway House, 474-476 Fulham Rd, SW6 1BY (020-7610 3137; http://broadwaylondon.com; Fulham Broadway tube; see website for opening hours).

The Club at Café Royal

Founded in 1865 by wine merchant Daniel Nicholas Thévenon, the Grade I listed Café Royal was the first gourmet French restaurant in Britain – boasting the most acclaimed wine list in the world – and was a honeypot for the rich and famous for some 150 years. The Club at Café Royal is the latest landmark in this enduring tradition, with a number of grand entertaining, dining and drinking spaces, as well as the hotel's spa, restaurant and bars.

Members are actively encouraged to work from the Club and use the premises as their headquarters, while enjoying a programme of events ranging from cutting-edge performances to inspiring lectures.

The Club at Café Royal, Hotel Café Royal, 68 Regent St, W1B 4DY (020-7406 3370; www. clubcaferoyal.com; Piccadilly Circus tube; see website for opening hours).

The Club at The Ivy

This fashionable club occupies the three floors above The Ivy restaurant in London's Theatreland and attracts members from the creative industries and arts. Opened in 2008, its design (by Martin Brudnizki) takes inspiration from The Ivy's Art Deco décor and offers an uber-stylish space in which to work, relax and socialise.

The Drawing Room – lined with a carefully selected library of books – serves breakfast, lunch, an early-bird theatre menu and dinner, while the Piano Bar is a comfortable meeting place by day and buzzy bar by night. The Loft on the top floor is a contemporary office space and also the venue for members' events such as quizzes, celebrity interviews, art shows, documentary screenings and cocktail parties.

The Club at The Ivy, 9 West St, WC2H 9NE (020-7557 6095; www.the-ivyclub.co.uk; Leicester Sq tube; see website for opening hours).

L'Escargot Upstairs Club

Housed in a magnificent Georgian townhouse in Soho dating from 1741 – once the private residence of the Duke of Portland – L'Escargot is London's oldest French restaurant. Established in 1927, it was the first in the UK to serve snails and its French bourgeois cuisine is legendary. L'Escargot is now under the control of Laurence Isaacson (co-founder of Groupe Chez Gerard) and Brian Clivaz (previously of the Arts Club and Home House), who restored the building to its former glory in 2014 and created a private members' club.

The L'Escargot Upstairs Club Privé (above the restaurant) is a haven for lovers of food, art and wine, occupying six eccentrically-designed rooms, including an elegant green dining room, a dark and inviting library complete with open fire, several smaller rainbow-hued working/networking areas, and a red lamp-lit boudoir. The jewel in the crown is the large, bright, barrel-vaulted salon, complete with baby grand piano. Each space is liberally sprinkled with classic and contemporary art, from Dali to Grayson Perry. There are also plans for a roof terrace.

The club is quite bohemian and laid back with no dress code. It expects members to have a liberal attitude to the arts and sciences and be amusing, interesting, 'nice' people who aren't rude to waiters and want the music turned up only slightly louder than at home!

L'Escargot Club, 48 Greek St, W1D 4EF (020-7439 7474; www.lescargot.co.uk/upstairs; Tottenham Court Rd tube; see website or contact for opening hours).

Grace Belgravia

London's first private members' club exclusively for women, Grace Belgravia occupies a historic (Grade II listed) building – a stunning 11,500ft^2 light-filled space with a spectacular double-height atrium. Firmly focused on health and wellbeing, it was created by Kate Percival, Chris O'Donaghue and Timothy Evans (the Queen's doctor) and named after the Three Graces of Greek mythology: goddesses of charm, beauty and creativity.

Preventative medicine and the art of ageing well informs every aspect of Grace, from the integrated medical clinic to the gorgeous spa retreat, fitness studio (with personal trainer), health-food restaurant and cosy bar. Whether you're looking for a GP, acupuncture, bio-identical hormone therapy, colonic hydrotherapy, genetic testing, physiotherapy or simply a pick-me-up, Grace's team of expert doctors, practitioners, nutritionists and therapists are at your service.

There's also a dynamic events and networking programme with a focus on the arts, fashion, culture, current affairs, health and wellbeing. In the evenings, Grace becomes the perfect Belgravia dinner venue, a cultural salon alive with cuisine, cocktails and camaraderie. Several times a month you can also feed your mind with an eclectic concoction of debate, art, music and other cultural events. Indulgent, exclusive – and reassuringly expensive.

Grace Belgravia, 11C West Halkin St, SW1X 8JL (020-7235 8900; www.gracebelgravia.com; Knightsbridge tube; see website for opening times).

The Groucho Club

Founded in 1985 as a response to Britain's (then) draconian licensing laws, the Groucho Club (named after Groucho Marx) in Soho was one of London's original arts and media private members' clubs, open to both sexes. It's a spacious, informal club on several floors with two restaurants, bars, lounges, private event rooms and 20 bedrooms for members and their guests.

At first glance the Groucho isn't much to write home about, but the understated décor, confusing corridors, lack of ostentation and superb contemporary art collection (mostly donated), are all part of the identity. A timeless classic and favourite of the city's glitterati, the Groucho is as rebellious as it gets in London's club world with a somewhat dark and edgy atmosphere.

The Groucho Club, 45 Dean St, W1D 4QB (020-7439 4685; www.thegrouchoclub.com; Leicester Sq tube; Mon-Fri 7.30-2am, Sat 8-2am, Sun 8am-10pm).

Home House

Home House occupies a trio of elegant Georgian townhouses in Portman Square. They were designed by James Wyatt in 1773, and the contrast between their Robert Adam interiors and the touches of cutting-edge minimalism added by the late Zaha Hadid makes Home House one of London's most stunning private clubs. It's the archetypal home from home with a restaurant, bars, nightclub, smoking lounge, intimate courtyard garden, boardroom, health and fitness club, boutique spa, 20 elegant bedrooms/suites, and a broad calendar of social events.

Nos 19-21 Portman Square have been home to, among others, Earl Grey (of tea fame) and spy Anthony Blunt, and today Home House appeals to people from all cultures, backgrounds and walks of life.

Home House, 20 Portman Sq, W1H 6LW (020-7670 2000; http://homehouse.co.uk; Marble Arch tube; see website for opening hours).

The Hospital Club

Aunique private members' club catering to folk in the creative industries, the Hospital Club in Covent Garden was founded by Paul Allen (co-founder of Microsoft) and Dave Stewart (Eurythmics) and opened in 2004. It occupies a seven-storey building – the former St Paul's Hospital, hence the name – and has 60,000ft^2 of space, including an award-winning TV and music studio, an art gallery, restaurant and bars, screening room and a live performance space. The club also encompasses a luxury boutique hotel

(opened in 2015) with 15 rooms and suites, which can also be booked by non-members and provide full access to the club's facilities.

The club offers a carefully selected schedule of members' events including writers' salons, masterclasses, talks, networking drinks' sessions and more. There are also live performances in the Oak Room, including music, comedy, spoken word, magic and cabaret, plus an outstanding art programme showcasing the best in rising talent and established artists, with exclusive private viewings for members. With an average of 40 events, exhibitions, social gatherings, live performances and around 60 film screenings each month, the Hospital Club is one of London's most vibrant creative communities.

Membership also provides reciprocal access to a clubs in cities around the world, including Buenos Aires, Madrid, Munich, New York, Shanghai and many more.

The Hospital Club, 24 Endell St, WC2H 9HQ (020-7170 9100; www.thehospitalclub.com; Covent Gdn tube; Mon-Fri 7-2am, Sat 8-2am, Sun 8am-9pm).

The House of St Barnabas Club

The intriguingly named House of St Barnabas is where social enterprise meets social interaction. It incorporates a dynamic, not-for-profit private members' club created to assist homeless people to get into work. Its benevolent roots stretch back to 1862 when it became home to the House of Charity – founded to help the homeless – and it operated as a hostel until 2006.

The 'House' is a beautiful restored (Grade I listed) Georgian building dating from 1746, boasting splendid Rococo plasterwork, chandeliers and silk-lined walls. The vibrant club features a European brasserie, alfresco dining, a secluded courtyard and chapel, a bar and lounge spaces. It also showcases a permanent art collection.

The House of St Barnabas, 1 Greek St, W1D 4NQ (020-7437 1894; https://hosb.org.uk; Tottenham Court Rd tube; Mon-Fri 8-1am, Sat noon-1am, closed Sundays).

Kensington Roof Gardens Club

Situated on top of the former Derry & Toms department store building on Kensington High Street, the spectacular 1.5 acre Kensington Roof Gardens are a world away from the hustle and bustle of London. Sir Richard Branson's rooftop oasis comprises three distinct gardens (Spanish, Tudor and an English walled garden), complete with flamingos and incomparable views over London. It also hosts the Babylon restaurant and a members' club.

The club is one of the city's most glamorous, offering an unrivalled line up of events throughout the year – from top DJs and live music to exclusive VIP experiences. Non-members can visit the gardens and dine at the restaurant.

Kensington Roof Gardens Club, 99 Kensington High St, W8 5SA (020-7937 7994; www.virginlimitededition.com/en/the-roof-gardens; High St Kensington tube; Fri-Sat 10pm-2am).

The Library

Founded by Ronald Ndoro in 2013 and designed by Marc Peridis, The Library is an exquisite and exclusive private members' club housed in a five-storey townhouse in Covent Garden, including a restaurant, bars, wellness hub and six

luxury hotel rooms. There's also a library (of course!), lounge, boardroom, smoking terrace, private dining facilities and 24-hour concierge.

Wellness is an important focus of the club, which offers meditation and mindfulness alongside intensive 45-minute fitness classes to set you up for the day. These are complemented by nutrition advice, personal trainers, body composition tests and classes such as yoga, Pilates, boxercise, dance fit and more. The club has been designed as a hub of creativity and innovation, and draws inspiration from literature, theatre, local community and sustainable design. There's a full programme of events and cultural engagements including live music, art exhibitions, film screenings, author-led book clubs and special talks.

Non-members can book hotel rooms, eat in the restaurant, and obtain a day pass allowing them to use all the club's facilities, including attending events (members can purchase up to three additional day passes for guests).

The Library, Martin's, 112 St Martin's Ln, WC2N 4BD (020-3302 7912; www.library.com; Leicester Sq tube; Mon-Fri 7-1am, Sat 11-1am, closed Sundays).

Quo Vadis Club

Occupying an upper floor in an elegant 18th-century building in which (it's said) Karl Marx wrote much of *Das Kapital*, Quo Vadis (the club) is an offshoot of Quo Vadis restaurant, a Soho landmark owned by Sam and Eddie Hart. With the focus very much on dining, drinking and revelry, the club hosts the good and the great of Soho in stylish, homely surroundings, with an open fire and live piano music adding to the atmosphere.

The QV website claims the club is 'a fine bolthole where you can meet for coffee, elevenses, lunch, meetings, dinner, drinks and a myriad of other delights'. It has an eclectic membership with the emphasis on members' 'individuality and charm'.

Quo Vadis Club, 26-29 Dean St, W1D 3LL (020-7437 9585; www.quovadissoho.co.uk/ club; Tottenham Court Rd tube; see website or contact for opening hours).

Searcys, The Gherkin

If you're aiming for the top, then you can do a lot worse than join Searcys – it's London's highest private members' club, located near the top of the Gherkin (see page 30) in the heart of the City. The club occupies the 38th floor of this distinctive building, just beneath the fine-dining restaurant and elegant bar, offering unparalleled views of London.

Membership gives you exclusive access to the club lounge, where breakfast is served in the morning and light dishes throughout the day, and priority bookings for the restaurant and bar. There's also a concierge service and exclusive members' events. The dome of the Gherkin is a unique and luxurious setting in which to conduct business or socialise with friends.

Searcys, The Gherkin, 30 St Mary Axe, EC3A 8EP (020-7071 5025; http://searcys.co.uk/venues/the-gherkin/searcys-club-the-gherkin; Aldgate tube; Mon-Fri 7.30am-11pm).

Soho House, Soho

A fast-growing chain of private members' clubs established in 1995, Soho House already numbers six London clubs plus another seven (and counting) in the UK and worldwide; we have chosen to feature the Dean Street 'House', situated in a Grade II listed townhouse built in 1732 and restored following a fire in 2009.

Originally established as a home from home for those working in the creative fields, Soho House attracts the majority of its members from industries such as film, fashion, advertising, music, art and the media. The Dean Street club is set over four floors with a courtyard, club bar, house kitchen, sitting room and a basement cinema and bar. The 43-seat cinema is air-conditioned and offers a varied programme of advance screenings and new releases.

Just a few doors away, the Dean Street Townhouse boutique hotel and all-day dining room is also owned by Soho House.

There are two types of membership (with discounted rates for under 27s): Local House gives you access to the space and facilities at Soho House Dean Street (and Greek Street, due to reopen in 2018), while Every House membership provides access to all Soho House clubs in London, the UK and abroad.

Soho House, 76 Dean St, W1D 3SG (020-3006 0076; www.sohohousedeanstreet.com; Tottenham Court Rd tube; Mon-Fri 7.30-1am, Sat 10-1am, Sun 10am-11pm).

South Kensington Club

Housed in Francis Bacon's former home and studio, the South Kensington Club (SKC) brings together a mix of 'interesting and interested' individuals, united by their passion for healthy food, wellness… and adventure. The club offers world-class fitness facilities along with a variety of complimentary therapies and treatments, both modern and traditional.

You can challenge your body in the state-of-the-art gym; indulge in skin treatments and spa rituals; or relax in the bathhouse with its Turkish *hamam*, Russian *banya* (steam bath) and a salt-water *watsu* pool. Other treats include a restaurant serving organic Mediterranean food and a tea library with a 'tea sommelier'.

The SKC hosts workshops, lectures and live music, but its most innovative idea is the Voyager Club which is designed to appeal to your inner Bear Grylls. Led by arctic adventurer Christina Franco, the Voyager Club encourages members to push boundaries, open their minds and do something different with their time; you can join one of its organised explorations, prepare for your own bucket-list expedition or just chill out and daydream in the Voyager Club Room (or basecamp).

Destinations are presented through

dinner parties, salon-style speaker events and practical workshops, while experts include adventurers such as long-distance swimmer Lewis Pugh and Kenyan wildlife conservationist Saba Douglas-Hamilton.

South Kensington Club, 38-42 Harrington Rd, SW7 3ND (020-3006 6868; www. southkensingtonclub.com; S Kensington tube; Mon-Fri 6.45am-midnight, Sat 8am-midnight, Sun 11am-11pm).

6.

Fitness Centres & Spas

Whether they're labelled health clubs, gyms, leisure centres, dance studios, baths, lidos or spas, in London you're spoilt for choice when it comes to losing weight, getting fit or pampering yourself. This chapter covers a whole gamut of choices; from boutique fitness studios for yummy mummies to kick-ass gyms for muscle men; dynamic dance studios to state-of-the-art fitness centres; and ravishing Art Deco swimming pools to luxurious, hedonistic spas.

London also has many excellent leisure centres, often council-run, which offer affordable well-equipped gyms, sports facilities, pools and treatment rooms, plus a wide range of classes. And there are a surprising number of beautiful (many Art Deco) outdoor lidos in London parks.

The choice can be daunting when choosing a gym and there many factors to take into account, such as cleanliness, staff know-how, range and quality of equipment, variety of classes, spa facilities and so forth. Ambience is important, too, with some private clubs displaying more nightclub glamour than sweatbox grit. Costs vary hugely; private clubs can be eye-wateringly expensive, while local leisure centres are a bargain. You don't have to commit yourself to a year's membership (and only go twice) as many gyms allow you to pay-as-you-go. So there's no excuse for not being fit in London!

1Rebel

One of London's best gyms for a serious kick-ass workout, 1Rebel specialises in high-intensity fitness sessions. A session in one of 1Rebel's 'fitness boutiques' (there's a second branch in Broadgate) is like working out in a high-end nightclub: subdued lighting, stripped industrial-style interiors, exposed brick and copper piping – and tons of high-tech equipment.

There are spacious changing facilities and lockers (stocked with luxury grooming and skincare products), sports-luxe retail fashion zones, and post-grind sustenance courtesy of Roots & Bulbs' cold-pressed juice bar (all food is gluten- and sugar-free).

1Rebel offers just three class types: Reshape (HIIT – high intensity interval training), Ride (spinning) and Rumble

(boxercise). The signature Reshape class is a breathless 45 minutes of high-intensity cardio on super high-tech running machines (Woodway 4Front treadmills), combined with bench work, to a soundtrack of the latest dance beats. Not for the faint-hearted, but highly addictive for fitness freaks.

1Rebel operates a no-contract 'pay-as-you-train' model. A session costs £20 and there are discounts if you book five or more. They come with complimentary sweat and shower towels and bottled water and, if you're doing a 30-minute lunchtime session, you also get a complimentary shake or juice.

1Rebel, 63 St Mary Axe, EC3A 8LE (020-3714 0710; www.1rebel.co.uk; Liverpool St tube/rail; Mon-Fri 6.30am-9pm, Sat 7.30am-1.30pm, Sun 7.30am-12.30pm).

Barrecore

The brainchild of Niki Rein, Barrecore's Chelsea studio opened in 2011 and was one of the first to bring the barre-based fitness regime from the US to the UK. A combination of ballet, Pilates and yoga, it combines fat-burning interval training with stretching – to improve muscle tone and flexibility – in a high-energy, low-impact workout. Be prepared to ache!

It's not the cheapest route to fitness – Barrecore offers an introductory class for £20 but regular classes cost £28, with discounts if you book a package – but if you want to rub shoulders with Chelsea's A-list yummy mummies and get super supple, then this is the place for you.

Barrecore, First Floor, Atlantic Ct, 77 King's Rd, SW3 4NX (020-7349 7500; www.barrecore.co.uk; Sloane Sq tube; Mon-Thu 6.30am-8.30pm, Fri 6.30am-7.30pm, Sat-Sun 9am-3pm).

Barry's Bootcamp

Famous for helping Hollywood's models and starlets cultivate their size-zero physiques, this hard-core fitness regime is now available in Euston (and EC2). The innovative technique is brutal but effective, boosting cardiovascular capacity, building muscle and burning some 1,000 calories in a single session.

The signature hour-long workouts take place in the 'dungeon' – a huge low-lit room – and include 25-30 minutes each of cardio-treadmill routines and strength training, utilising free weights, resistance bands, medicine balls and other equipment. All for £20! Different body parts and muscle groups are targeted by different trainers on different days, so each class offers something unique.

Barry's Bootcamp, 163 Euston Rd, NW1 2BH (020-7387 7001; www.barrysbootcamp.com; Euston tube/rail; Mon-Thu 5.45am-10.30pm, Fri 5.45am-9.30pm, Sat 7am-8.30pm, Sun 7am-7pm).

Baths & Lidos

London Fields Lido

There are a great many swimming pools, baths and open-air lidos in London, both public and private, which are excellent value and don't require membership (although members receive discounts). Our favourites are featured below:

Brockwell Lido (Brockwell Park, Dulwich Rd, SE24 0PA; 020-7274 3088; www.brockwelllido.com; Brixton tube or Herne Hill rail) is an Art Deco classic. The 50-metre pool first opened in July 1937; restored to its former glory in the '90s (with a gym and an excellent café) it's now open year round.

Ironmonger Row Baths (1 Norman St, EC1V 3AA; 020-3642 5520; www.better.org.uk/leisure/ironmonger-row-baths; Old St tube/rail) opened in 1931 as a washhouse and was recently restored at a cost of £16.5 million. Among its delights are a blissful spa (three hot rooms, two saunas, two steam rooms, an ice-cold plunge pool and more), alongside two pools and a gym – all at leisure-centre prices.

London Fields Lido (London Fields West Side, Hackney, E8 3EU; 020-7254 9038; www.better.org.uk/leisure/london-fields-lido; London Fields rail) in Hackney is the city's only 50-metre heated outdoor pool, open all year round. It features two cafés, a large sundeck and a sunbathing area.

Marshall Street Leisure Centre (15 Marshall St, W1F 7EL; 0333-005 0417; www.everyoneactive.com/centre/marshall-street-leisure-centre; Oxford Circus tube) is built around a historic 30-metre pool, dating from 1931 and beautifully restored (the centre is Grade II listed). There's also a 100-station gym, exercise/dance studios and a day spa.

Tooting Bec Lido (Tooting Bec Rd, SW16 1RU; 020-8871 7198; www.placesforpeopleleisure.org/centres/tooting-bec-lido; Streatham rail) opened as a bathing lake in 1906 and is the largest freshwater swimming pool in England. Club members can swim all year round.

Marshall Sreet

Core Collective

A sleek new gym in Kensington founded by City trader turned fitness guru Jason de Savary, Core Collective is one of a new breed of boutique gyms which have reinvented the way Londoners exercise. It's a spacious high-tech gym with low, multi-coloured lighting, lively thumping music and a variety of high-intensity signature workouts. The 45-minute classes offer something for everyone including Velocity (HIIT), Accelerate (spinning), Resistance (suspension training or TRX), Sculpt (dance), plus power yoga and Pilates (and the obligatory juice bar/café).

With no sign-up fees, no contract and no monthly charges, Core Collective offers the flexibility to come and go with no strings attached.

Core Collective, 45 Phillimore Walk, W8 7RZ (020-7937 6377; https://core-collective.co.uk; High St Kensington tube; Mon-Fri 6.15am-9pm, Sat 8am-5pm, Sun 9am-3pm).

Danceworks

One of the world's leading dance studios, Danceworks was established in 1982 and is housed in a Victorian building opposite Selfridges with 11 multi-purpose studios. It offers a wide variety of accessible dance classes at all levels, including ballet, street, world dance and tap, plus fitness, Pilates, martial arts and even singing classes, many taught by professionals from the dance and entertainment industry. Although you need to be a member, classes are reasonably priced and are run on a drop-in basis (until the class is full). Danceworks also holds regular masterclasses and workshops taught by top companies, dancers and choreographers.

Once you're all danced out, there's an in-house complementary therapy centre, Natureworks, offering everything from massage and osteopathy to acupuncture and life coaching.

Danceworks, 16 Balderton St, W1K 6TN (020-7629 6183; http://danceworks.net; Bond St tube; Mon-Fri 8am-10pm, Sat-Sun 9am-6pm).

Equinox

A chain of five-star super gyms favoured by (ex) President Barack Obama, Equinox was rated America's best gym by *Fitness Magazine*. Its flagship London location is housed in the historic Art Deco Derry & Toms building in Kensington (once home to fashion powerhouse Biba), where the dramatic exercise room features an illuminated elliptical glass skylight and the studios are designed by Keith Hobbs, the man behind the interiors at the Nobu restaurant chain

Equinox offers a wide range of fitness classes, Pilates, personal training and spa sessions, and has everything you need to get in shape. There's even an anti-gravity machine to analyse and correct your gait!

Equinox, 99 Kensington High St, W8 5SA (020-7666 6000; www.equinox.com/clubs/london/kensington; Kensington High St tube; Mon-Fri 6am-10pm, Sat-Sun 8am-9pm).

Evolve Wellness Centre

Established by Corrine Blum, a ballerina and choreographer from San Francisco, and entrepreneur Adrian Kowal, the Evolve Wellness Centre in South Kensington offers

a variety of treatments for body, mind and soul, including an extensive choice of yoga and Pilates classes, holistic natural therapies, innovative lifestyle workshops and educational courses. Whether your focus is fitness, weight loss, reducing stress or improving your well-being, Evolve can provide you with the tools to reach your goals.

There's a range of packages on offer, including drop-in classes and annual membership. You can also sign up for workshops, courses, treatments and a dedicated weight-loss programme.

Evolve Wellness Centre, 10 Kendrick Mews, SW7 3HG (020-7581 4090; www.evolvewellnesscentre. com; S Kensington tube; see website for opening times).

Frame Shoreditch

Opened in 2009 by New Zealanders Pip Black and Joan Murphy in two converted railway arches in Shoreditch, upbeat Frame (now with three other branches) is a gym with a difference. Rather than just doing their own thing pounding a treadmill, clients are encouraged to take part in feel-good, fun-filled classes. Membership starts from £65 a month or you can pay as you go.

The Shoreditch Frame has five studios: a 'hard core' fitness room (complete with punch pads, TRX, bikes and plyometric boxes), a yoga studio, a reformer Pilates studio, and two large studios serving up a mixture of fitness, Frame Signature and dance classes. There's a 'Fuel bar' for fresh juices, smoothies, snacks and coffee, too.

Frame Shoreditch, 29 New Inn Yd, EC2A 3EY (020-7033 1855; https://moveyourframe.com; Shoreditch High St rail; Mon-Fri 6.30am-10pm, Sat 8.30am-6pm, Sun 9am-6.30pm).

Golden Lane Sport & Fitness

Located in a Grade II listed building, part of which was once used as jail cells, Golden Lane in the heart of the City offers a high-tech gym, a 20-metre rooftop pool, indoor badminton courts, and outdoor courts for tennis and netball. There are a variety of energetic and relaxing activities, sessions and courses for all ages and abilities, including martial arts classes (karate, taekwondo and judo), and 30-minute power classes at lunchtimes and after work.

Golden Lane offers excellent value for money, either pay-per-visit or membership, and offers a decent discount if you locally.

Golden Lane Sport & Fitness, Fann St, EC1Y 0SH (020-7250 1464; www.goldenlanefitness. com; Barbican tube; Mon-Fri 6am-10pm, Sat-Sun 8am-6pm).

Gymbox

Offering some of London's most original workouts, Gymbox in Covent Garden (there are eight across the capital) was one of the first to combine the atmosphere of a nightclub with state-of-the-art fitness facilities. With legions of treadmills, cross trainers and bikes, free weight areas, an Olympic-sized boxing ring, combat rooms, spinning room, dance studios, resident DJs and over 100 classes a week, Gymbox is bursting with options.

The various studios feature everything from holistic yoga and Pilates-based exercises to more energetic sessions, including a fantastic 'rave' dance class and one that involves pummelling a punch bag in time to music. There's also a sauna and steam room to help soothe aching muscles.

Gymbox, 42-49 St Martins Ln, WC2N 4EJ (020-7395 0270; http://gymbox.com; Leicester Sq tube; Mon-Fri 6am-11pm, Sat-Sun 10am-6pm).

Jubilee Hall

One of central London's best and most affordable gyms, Jubilee Hall in vibrant Covent Garden is a sun-lit warehouse gym featuring a huge open area packed with high-tech cardio machines – treadmills, cross-trainers, bikes and steppers – from Matrix Fitness with interactive screens. If you prefer classes there's hatha yoga, Pilates, burlesque and flamenco, spinning, circuits, and classes from Les Mills, the leading name in structured fitness programmes. There are also great personal trainers, free weights, a sauna and more.

You can take out no-contract membership which gives you access to over 100 other centres in London and the southeast; non-members are welcome on daily rates, And there's a café with free wi-fi.

Jubilee Hall, 30 The Piazza, WC2E 8BE (020-7836 4007; www.jubileehalltrust.org/jubilee-hall; Covent Gdn tube; Mon-Fri 6.45am-10pm, Sat 9am-9pm, Sun 10am-5pm).

KX Gym & Spa

Much more than just a gym, the luxurious KX is an exclusive private members' club incorporating a gym, exercise classes, spa, nail lounge, clubroom and restaurant. It's achingly trendy – the changing rooms are fitted out with saunas, steam rooms and plunge pools – and offers a bespoke approach to fitness, health and wellbeing. Classes and personal training sessions take in strength and conditioning, fat loss, barre, Pilates (mat and reformer), yoga, dojo, kickboxing, boxing, spinning and more. And you're likely to be panting and sweating alongside celebrities such as Gwyneth Paltrow and Kylie Minogue.

The downside to such a glam gym is it costs £2,000 to join, and membership is a breath-taking £6,000 a year! But at least you don't pay extra for classes.

KX Gym & Spa, 151 Draycott Ave, SW3 3AL (020-7584 5333; www.kxlife.co.uk; S Kensington tube; Mon-Fri 6.30am-10.30pm, Sat 8am-10.30pm, Sun 8am-8pm).

The Library

The brainchild of Zana Morris, The Library is a beautiful private members' training club housed in a former synagogue in leafy Notting Hill. Set among velvet sofas and designer wallpapers is a variety of serious high-tech machines designed to work various muscle groups to exhaustion. The club offers a science-based workout based on High Intensity Training (HIT) – short, intense 15-minute periods of weights and abs reps at least three times a week – alongside supplements and a nutritional programme, which it's claimed result in improved muscle tone, fat loss and increased overall fitness.

The Library also offers chilled yoga, strengthening barre or stress-busting boxing classes, luxury changing rooms and relaxation areas, including a private garden, pool tables and reading nooks.

The Library, 206-208 Kensington Park Rd, W11 1NR (020-7221 7992; www.thelibrarygym.com; Ladbroke Grove tube; Mon-Fri 6am-8.30pm, Sat-Sun 8.30am-2pm).

Pineapple Dance Studios

Established by Debbie Moore in 1979 in Covent Garden, Pineapple Dance Studios is the UK's most famous dance school – it's where dancer-turned-celebrity Louie Spence used to work. There are over ten studios of various sizes on four floors offering everything from tap and Latin to jazz and street dance, ballet and salsa to Egyptian and hip-hop – a total of around 20 dance styles and over 250 classes a week. If you can dance it, they do it here.

You need to be a member but all classes are on a drop-in basis – costing from £6 to £15 (most are £7-£8) – and you don't need to book.

Pineapple Dance Studios, 16 Langley St, WC2H 9JA (020-7836 4006; www.pineapple.uk.com; Covent Gdn tube; Mon-Fri 8.30am-10pm, Sat 9am-6.30pm, Sun 10am-6pm).

The Porchester Centre & Spa

Work up a sweat or simply relax at the Porchester Centre in Bayswater, a beautiful Art Deco (1929, Grade II

listed) building, which houses Porchester Hall and Porchester Spa. The centre offers a wide range of facilities, including a 140-station gym, exercise studios, two swimming pools, squash court – and a luxurious spa. Men and women can use the spa on alternate days, with mixed use on Sundays from 4-10pm.

The spa (voted London's best-value by *The Sunday Times*) is an oasis of calm, with two Russian steam rooms, three Turkish hot rooms, a traditional Finnish sauna, an ice-cold plunge pool and specialities such as *schmeissing*, a vigorous traditional (men-only) Jewish form of massage.

Porchester Centre, Queensway, W2 5HS (020-7313 3858; www.everyoneactive. com/centre/porchester-spa or www. porchesterspatreatments.co.uk; Royal Oak tube; daily 10am-10pm).

Speedflex

Aunique training and fitness method, Speedflex offers high-intensity, low-impact circuit training using specially-designed machines. Heart-rate monitors provide real-time results for effort and performance levels, as well as a detailed summary (including calorie count) at the end. Speedflex machines calculate resistance based on the force applied, which means that the intensity of your workout is significantly higher, leading to increased calorie burn.

The design of the machine, which uses hydraulics to create concentrically based forces so that muscles won't tear, means users experience little or no post-exercise muscle soreness. Traditional exercise aids such as power bags, medicine balls and kettle bells also feature in a typical session.

Speedflex, Plough Court, 33-36 Lombard St, EC3V 9BQ (0844-543 3631; http://speedflex.com/ speedflex-centres/city-of-london; Monument tube; Mon-Fri 7am-8pm, closed Sat-Sun).

The Third Space

This highly-regarded luxury gym and health club in Soho looks like something from the set of *Star Wars*. It's laid out over four floors and is high-tech heaven for fitness freaks: there are energy crystals embedded in the walls, glass ceilings (and floors), a state-of-the-art cardio gym, a carbon-filtered 20-metre swimming pool, a sky-lit climbing wall, a Pilates and Gyrotonic

studio, a padded martial arts dojo and more. There's even an altitude training (hypoxic chamber) room.

Members have access to some 130 classes a week, as well as a gym kit laundry service, sauna and steam rooms, wi-fi, a juice bar, a medical centre offering complementary therapies and a live DJ.

There are sister branches in Canary Wharf, Marylebone and Tower Bridge.

The Third Space, 67 Brewer St, W1F 9US (020-7439 6333; www.thirdspace.london/soho; Piccadilly Circus tube; Mon-Fri 6.30am-11pm, Sat-Sun 8.30am-8.30pm).

YMCA Club

This super-gym is part of Central YMCA, which was the world's first YMCA (Young Men's Christian Association) and is now a leading UK health and fitness and education charity. The YMCA was founded

in London in 1844 and expanded across the planet to become the world's largest youth movement, offering a unique and ever-evolving range of training, qualifications, skills and services.

The YMCA Club is the largest health and fitness facility in central London, offering an abundance of high-tech resistance machines, cardio equipment and training apparatus, along with a high standard of professional instruction, personal trainers, and sports and beauty therapies - for allcomers (not just men).

Facilities include a two-tiered cardio zone, a dedicated free weights room, a state-of-the-art Stott Pilates studio, six exercise studios, a 25-metre swimming pool, three badminton courts, and a sauna and steam room. There are over 125 classes a week, including aerobics, sculpt, yoga, Zumba, spinning, TRX, circuits, Pilates, kettlebells, martial arts, barre and more, all of which are included in the low membership fees, which start from under £50 a month. There's also a café and lounge where you can relax after your workout.

Central YMCA, 112 Great Russell St, WC1B 3NQ (0370-218 8590; www.ymcaclub.co.uk; Tottenham Court Rd tube; Mon-Fri 6.30am-10.30pm, Sat 9am-8.30pm, Sun 9am-7pm).

York Hall Leisure Centre

Housed in a splendid neo-Georgian (Grade II listed) building opened in 1929 by the Duke of York, York Hall Leisure Centre in Bethnal Green is one of East London's hidden gems. Originally opened as a Turkish bathhouse, the

hall later established itself as the home of British boxing. Today it features a high-tech gym, group exercise facilities, two indoor swimming pools (including a 33-metre pool), an award-winning spa and a café.

The gym is fully equipped with the latest Technogym equipment, including cardiovascular machines such as treadmills and rowers, resistance equipment (including free weights) and dedicated stretching areas, along with fitness aids such as Swiss balls. There is also a wide range of fitness classes such as Boxfit, circuits and Zumba, alongside ever-popular Pilates and yoga.

York Hall Day Spa opened (as Spa London) in 2005 and was the city's first public-sector day spa. While not as luxurious as a 5-star hotel spa, it offers an authentic affordable spa experience. Occupying the beautifully restored former Turkish baths, the spa combines the best traditional thermal therapies with the latest modern spa treatments, including a relaxing three-hour thermal Spa Experience costing around £26.

York Hall offers a range of affordable membership options to suit every budget, from pay and play and short-term passes to monthly or annual prepaid membership.

York Hall Leisure Centre, 5 Old Ford Rd, E2 9PJ (020-8980 2243; www.better.org.uk/leisure/york-hall-leisure-centre; Bethnal Grn tube; Mon-Fri 7am-9.30pm, Sat 8am-8.30pm, Sun 8am-7.30pm).

7.

Hotels

The 20 million international visitors who descend on London each year have a vast choice of places to stay, from magnificent five-star palaces and chic designer boutiques to pared-down budget hotels and cosy B&Bs. Once dominated by opulent grand hotels such as Claridge's, The Dorchester and The Ritz, the capital's hotel scene has been revitalised in recent years by a new generation of hip hotels, featuring vibrant and user-friendly design, cutting-edge technology and individually-tailored creature comforts (such as your own choice of pillow).

Many London hotels feature world-class restaurants and bars (see **Chapter 1**) and some are a destination in their own right: visit the St Pancras Renaissance Hotel for its amazing interiors or the Mondrian on London's Southbank for its fabulous river views. Each of our selection of hotels – which encompasses all price brackets – offers something out of the ordinary, whether it's eccentricity, history, effortless chic or cutting-edge design, not forgetting the all-important value for money.

Some are a short distance away from the heaving tourist hotspots of central London, but it's well worth taking a few more tube stops to fresh and arty areas such as Bethnal Green, Camberwell, Hoxton or Shoreditch, to discover the parts of this amazing city where the cool dudes hang out.

Price Guide: £ = economy, ££ = moderate, £££ = expensive, ££££ = luxury

Ace Hotel

Previously a dowdy Crowne Plaza hotel, the Ace London has blossomed into one of trendy Shoreditch's hippest hangouts since being taken over by American company Ace in 2013. Comfortable, stylish and slightly bohemian, its standard rooms feature original artwork and vintage furniture alongside the usual flat-screen TV and minibar, while upgraded rooms include dining tables and daybeds – some even have retro turntables with vinyl records!

Social spaces include a lobby with communal tables, a bar and art gallery. There's also a snack bar, coffee shop, juice bar, brasserie, flower shop, basement bar with live music and DJs, as well as the obligatory gym. Ace is a cool place to sleep, eat and drink and, not surprisingly, attracts a young and fashionable crowd.

Ace Hotel, 100 Shoreditch High St, E1 6JQ (020-7613 9800; www.acehotel.com/london; Shoreditch High St rail; ££-£££).

The Artist Residence

A cosy boutique hotel in an elegant Regency townhouse designed by Thomas Cubitt, the award-winning Artist Residence opened in Pimlico in 2014. The welcoming façade, with smart red-and-white awnings, gives way to pared-down décor and lots of art: the hotel doubles as a gallery for a diverse range of urban, graphic and street artists.

There are just ten individually designed (air-conditioned) rooms and suites featuring rustic, custom-made furnishings and original art, plus (Smeg) minibar, flat-screen TV, radio and wi-fi. When you get the munchies, the casual-chic Cambridge Street Kitchen serves food all day – and you can relax in the cellar cocktail bar or games room (complete with ping-pong table).

The Artist Residence, 52 Cambridge St, SW1V 4QQ (020-7931 8946; http:// artistresidencelondon.co.uk; Victoria tube/rail; £££-££££).

The Beaumont

Located on a quiet garden square in Mayfair, the Beaumont is the first hotel from celebrated restaurateurs Corbin & King (the pair behind the Delaunay and Wolseley café-restaurants). Opened in 2014, this Art Deco-inspired five-star hotel occupies a stately 1926 building, and the dramatic interior design – chequerboard lobby floor, early 20th-century art, gleaming period antiques – is a tribute to its creators. It has 73 elegant rooms and suites featuring marble and chrome bathrooms, flat-screen TV, Nespresso machines and complimentary soft drinks.

Eating options include the sophisticated '30s-style Colony Grill Room, plus two elegant lounge bars and a spa complete with steam room, sauna and ice-cold plunge pool.

The Beaumont, Brown Hart Gdns, W1K 6TF (020-7499 1001; www.thebeaumont.com; Bond St tube; ££££).

The Boundary

A recent venture from Sir Terence Conran and Peter Prescott, the Boundary Project occupies a beautifully converted Victorian warehouse in edgy Shoreditch, comprising a boutique hotel, restaurants, bars, café, bakery and a delicatessen. The hotel has 12 elegant, contemporary guestrooms – each inspired by a legendary designer or design movement, from Young British to Bauhaus, Eileen Gray to Le Corbusier – plus five suites (including four duplexes) ranging from modern Dickensian to Chinoiserie.

You can eat British fare in the informal ground floor Albion café-restaurant, opt for classic French provincial cooking in the Boundary basement restaurant, or enjoy panoramic views in the award-winning Rooftop restaurant, which has a heated orangery, open fire pit and luxury blankets for chilly evenings.

The Boundary, 2-4 Boundary St, E2 7DD (020-7729 1051; www.theboundary.co.uk; Shoreditch High St rail; ££-£££).

Charlotte Street Hotel

Situated in bohemian Fitzrovia, the five-star Charlotte Street Hotel is a delightful pit stop for fans of early 20th-century art and literature. Designer Kit Kemp took inspiration for the hotel's design – a fusion of flowery English and avant-garde – from the Bloomsbury Group, and it features original art by members of this influential set, including Vanessa Bell, Duncan Grant and Roger Fry. The Oscar Brasserie is dominated by a three-wall mural reflecting scenes of London in 2000 painted in a distinctive Bloomsbury style.

flourishes: high ceilings, huge comfortable beds, polished granite and oak bathrooms combine with modern essentials such as flat-screen TVs, DVD players and iPod docking stations. The hotel's light and airy sweep of a lobby leads into the sumptuous and comfortable drawing room and library, each with French sandstone fireplaces and honour bars. There's also a fully-equipped gym, DVD library, screening room and film club.

The Charlotte Street Hotel epitomises contemporary London and is popular with Bloomsbury's modern-day media crowd who flock to Oscar's pewter bar to sip cocktails – try the rhubarb and lemon grass Bellini – or nibble at the all-day afternoon tea.

Formerly a dental hospital, the hotel has 52 rooms and 13 suites, which combine English understatement with bold

Charlotte Street Hotel, 15-17 Charlotte St, W1T 1RJ (020-7806 2000; www.firmdalehotels.com/london/charlotte-street-hotel; Goodge St tube; ££££).

Chiltern Firehouse Hotel

Occupying a converted neo-Gothic fire station dating from 1889, the five-star Chiltern Firehouse hotel in Marylebone was opened by hotelier André Balazs (owner of the Mercer in New York and the iconic Chateau Marmont in Hollywood) in 2013. The beautifully and sympathetically restored building offers 26 elegant bedrooms and suites with working fireplaces and generously appointed bathrooms. The well-heeled guests enjoy a private bar, 24-hour service and a personal concierge; a bedside note – 'Dial '0' for anything' – sums up the ethos perfectly.

As if that wasn't enough, the Chiltern Firehouse is also home to one of the city's most celebrated restaurants, led by Michelin-starred chef Nuno Mendes.

Chiltern Firehouse Hotel, 1 Chiltern St, W1U 7PA (020-7073 7676; www.chilternfirehouse.com; Baker St tube; ££££).

Church Street Hotel

A cool Latin-American oasis hidden away in Camberwell, south London, Church Street Hotel is one of the capital's most unique boutique hotels. Unashamedly kitsch, the 31 rooms are individually decorated, full of glorious bright Latin colours and throws, and funky tiled bathrooms

inspired by the warmth and sensuality of the Americas. This quirky exuberant hotel is a gem, offering excellent service, organic breakfasts and great value for money.

The Havana Lounge offers complimentary gourmet teas and Monmouth coffee or you can mix yourself a drink at the honesty bar, while the excellent basement Communion Bar offers artisan cocktails and live music. And Camberwell itself is one of London's buzziest neighbourhoods with a vibrant local art scene and nightlife.

Church Street Hotel, 29-33 Camberwell Church St, SE5 8TR (020-7703 5984; http://churchstreethotel.com; Denmark Hill rail; ££).

Citizen M, Bankside

A chic, affordable 192-room hotel on London's south bank close to the Tate Modern, Dutch-owned Citizen M is one of a new breed of hip hotels that have sprung up in recent years. The minimalist rooms have floor-to-ceiling windows, comfortable king-sized beds, cool lighting, air-con, powerful rain showers, touch-screen room controls,

flat-screen TVs with free movies, and free goodies in the fridge.

The theme is self-service. You check in via a touch screen and can chill out in the 'living room' and workspace area where there are glossy tomes on photography, fashion, travel and design, and free-to-use iMacs dotted around – with free wi-fi of course. And there's a cosy 24/7 self-service canteen/bar for breakfast, snacks and cocktails.

Citizen M, 20 Lavington St, SE1 0NZ (020-3519 1680; www.citizenm.com/destinations/london/ london-bankside-hotel; Southwark tube; £-££).

Good Hotel

F or a unique hotel experience look no further than the Good Hotel, a floating hotel located in Royal Victoria Dock, transported by barge from Holland in 2016. Unlike other hotels, the profits are ploughed back into the business, which offers training and jobs to local long-term unemployed people.

From the outside it looks like a giant, black shipping container, while inside the slick minimalist industrial design is offset by snug, dimly-lit corners with comfy sofas and communal tables in a large open plan 'living room' (bar, reception and library). There are 148 comfortable rooms (large and small), plus a rooftop bar, restaurant, meeting rooms, free wi-fi and more. However, it's the laid-back atmosphere and unique character that make this a special place.

Good Hotel, Royal Victoria Dock, Western Gateway E16 1FA (020-3637 7401; www. goodhotellondon.com; Royal Victoria DLR; £-££).

Hoxton Holborn

A hip hotel opened in 2014 in a former office block, Hoxton Holborn (from the same outfit as Hoxton Shoreditch) has 174 cleverly designed rooms with funky décor, en-suite bathrooms with rainfall showers, free wi-fi and international phone calls, large flat-screen TVs, and mini-fridges with complimentary milk and water. Rooms come in a range of sizes – Shoebox, Snug, Cosy and Roomy – and are good value for the location, including 'breakfast-in-a-bag' delivered to your room.

Reasonably-priced eating options include an all-day American-style grill, Hubbard & Bell (great steaks), the basement Chicken Shop (spit-roasted chicken) and the next-door coffee shop Holborn Grind, plus a lively lobby bar hosting weekly events.

Hoxton Holborn, 199-206 High Holborn, WC1V 7BD (020-7661 3000; https://thehoxton.com/london/holborn; Holborn tube; ££-££££).

The Laslett

A contemporary boutique hotel from Tracy Lowy and Living Rooms, the Laslett takes its name from Rhaune Laslett, founder of the Notting Hill Carnival. Located on a quiet street in trendy Notting Hill, the hotel comprises five elegant townhouses containing 51 delightful bedrooms and suites. Rooms feature designer furnishings from Pinch and Race, vintage knick-knacks, curated artworks, proper blankets and Neal's Yard Remedies in the bathrooms – plus Sky TV, a complimentary smartphone and Penguin Classics for bedtime reading.

The hotel lobby is a popular neighbourhood hangout, incorporating a lounge, library and designer boutique, and the Henderson bar and coffee shop serving breakfasts, evening cocktails and an irresistible array of signature dishes from local chef Sally Clarke.

The Laslett, 8 Pembridge Gdns, W2 4DU (020-7792 6688; www.living-rooms.co.uk/hotel/the-laslett; Notting Hill Gate tube; ££).

Mondrian Hotel

Inspired by the glamour of '20s Art Deco liners – a vast copper hull cuts through the centre of the building – the Mondrian (full name: Mondrian London at Sea Containers) is a striking contemporary five-star hotel on the south bank of the Thames designed by Tom Dixon. The 359 spacious rooms, suites and apartments feature bespoke furnishings and designer décor with all the usual facilities you would expect (flat-screen satellite TV, free wi-fi, luxury bathroom, etc.) plus unexpected touches such as a private ivy-clad patio or unobscured river view. There's also an excellent restaurant, elegant spa, fitness centre and cinema.

The Mondrian is home to two bars: the innovative Dandelyan (see page 16) and the rooftop Rumpus Room, which offers panoramic views over the city.

Mondrian Hotel, 20 Upper Ground, SE1 9PD (020-3747 1000; www.morganshotelgroup.com/ mondrian/mondrian-london/; Southwark tube; ££-££££).

My Hotel Chelsea

Opened in 1999 by Andreas Thrasyvoulou, My Hotel Chelsea is a contemporary four-star boutique hotel in west London (there's another in Bloomsbury). The quirky hotel features 46 bijou (but elegant) air-conditioned rooms and suites with free wi-fi, flat-screen TV, DVD player, minibar, a safe and excellent showers, plus wacky touches such as Sound Asleep pillows (on request) into which you can plug your iPod. There's also

a lounge-restaurant serving Italian dishes with a Sicilian flavour.

My Hotel offers a unique 'My Preferences' service and will endeavour to cater to your needs, whether you want a hypoallergenic duvet or a yoga mat for morning workouts, and can provide bespoke local recommendations (e.g. regarding places to eat or visit) based on your interests and preferences.

My Hotel Chelsea, 35 Ixworth Pl, SW3 3QX (020-7225 7500; http://myhotels.com/chelsea; S Kensington tube; ££).

The Portobello Hotel

A charmingly eccentric hotel with an international reputation as one of London's most exclusive hideaways, the Portobello Hotel is cutting edge but with an intimate homely feel, housed in two converted neo-classical mansions on a quiet street in Notting Hill. Opened in 1971, this four-star hotel has played host to many famous names from the world of music, show business and fashion, but nevertheless remains a pleasingly unpretentious place, with a more civilised demeanour than its reputation might suggest.

The 24 quirkily themed rooms are inventive, cosy and sensual, with all the usual modern conveniences such as air-conditioning, flat-screen TVs and free wi-fi; the charming basement Japanese water garden room has a wonderful spa bath, its own private grotto and a small garden. Some border on the eccentric: one

room has a spectacular Victorian bathing machine – a bizarre collection of copper pipes, taps and a massive sprinkler – attached to a turn-of-the-century claw-foot bath. The beds are sumptuous, some four-poster or, in the popular Round Room, circular.

In the afternoon and evening, the sitting room becomes somewhere to relax with a drink and enjoy the views over the private gardens. There's a light snack menu to accompany a selection of drinks from the well-stocked honesty bar.

The Portobello Hotel, 22 Stanley Gardens, W11 2NG (020-7727 2777; www.portobellohotel.com; Notting Hill Gate tube; £££).

Qbic London City

A chic budget hotel in Shoreditch in East London with capsule-style modular rooms, Qbic London City is handily situated for some of the city's best Asian food (the Indian and Bangladeshi restaurants of Brick Lane are close by), art galleries, boutiques, creative businesses and nightlife. And you can borrow a bicycle to help you explore.

The lobby resembles a living room with self-service check-in and a relaxed lounge/bar area, while the 171 compact, soundproofed rooms have a futuristic feel with comfortable double beds, urban art and murals, mood lighting, monsoon showers, smart TVs and free wi-fi. You can chill out in the relaxing common area and refuel in the bar-restaurant, which serves everything from coffee to cocktails.

Qbic London City, 42 Adler St, E1 1EE (020-3021 2644; https://qbichotels.com/london-city; Aldgate E tube; ££).

The Rookery Hotel

The Rookery Hotel in the City offers a delicious glimpse of a bygone age, with an atmosphere more redolent of a private club than a hotel, full of warmth and character, quirky but with state-of-the-art facilities. The homely interior boasts sumptuous Georgian detailing: polished wood panelling, stone-flagged floors, open fires and antique furniture.

The 33 en-suite rooms are furnished with antiques, some dating back to the 17th century, including carved oak or four-poster beds, beautiful carpets, original pictures, panelled walls and windows hung with heavy silk curtains, while stunning bathrooms have original Victorian fittings (some with free-standing roll-top baths) and huge showerheads. All rooms have air-conditioning, flat-screen TV, DVD player, iPod docking, mini bar, safe, desk and free wi-fi.

The Rookery Hotel, 12 Peter's Ln, Cowcross St, EC1M 6DS (020-7336 0931; www.rookeryhotel. com; Farringdon tube; ££-£££).

Rosewood Hotel

Occupying a magnificently restored grand Edwardian edifice dating from 1914, the five-star Rosewood Hotel, opened in 2013, is one of the city's most dramatic and luxurious hotels. The 262 well-appointed and spacious rooms (all are over 30m²) and 44 sumptuous suites combine original Belle Époque elements with contemporary designs (by Tony Chi) and  the finest materials – such as luxury Italian bedding and lovely marble bathrooms – furnished with huge flat-screen TVs, Nespresso coffee machines, sleek Geneva sound systems and iPod docks.

The hotel also boasts an acclaimed restaurant, the Holborn Dining Room, and a renowned bar (Scarfes – see page 22), plus the obligatory luxury spa and state-of-the-art fitness suite, a deli and an outdoor terrace.

Rosewood Hotel, 252 High Holborn, WC1V 7EN (020-7781 8888; www.rosewoodhotels.com/en/ London; Holborn tube; ££££).

Rough Luxe

A bijou boutique hotel comprising just 9 rooms in unprepossessing King's Cross, Rough Luxe – 'half rough, half luxury' – is one of the city's most idiosyncratic hotels. This Grade II listed townhouse was transformed by Rabih Hage in 2008 into a daring blend of old and new. Combining original art and beautiful fabrics with distressed walls and bare floorboards, the end result is a bold and lovely piece of design.

At Rough Luxe the luxury lies in the detail: guests may choose their preferred wine and bed linen, enjoy the finest hand-made toiletries and delicious breakfasts, and you can even bring your pet. And the welcome and service are second-to-none.

Rough Luxe, 1 Birkenhead St, WC1H 8BA (020-7837 5338; www.roughluxe.co.uk; King's Cross rail/tube; ££-£££).

St Martin's Lane Hotel

This sleek designer hotel was recently given a sensitive facelift by interior designer Tim Andreas – without losing the dramatic impact of the original 1999 interiors by Philippe Starck – and offers five-star comfort and stunning style in hip Covent Garden. The 204 luxurious rooms feature floor-to-ceiling windows, custom-made Philippe Starck furniture, mood lighting, high-tech media hubs, huge smart TVs, minibars and free wi-fi, while hotel amenities include free access to a gym (Gymbox), bike loans and a hair salon.

Public spaces include The Den, the hotel's eclectic lounge and hub, the highly-rated contemporary Asia de Cuba fusion restaurant, and a popular cutting-edge cocktail bar cum nightclub (Light Bar) featuring top DJs.

St Martin's Lane Hotel, 45 St Martin's Ln, WC2N 4HX (020-7300 5500; www.morganshotelgroup. com; Leicester Sq tube; £££).

St Pancras Renaissance Hotel

Opened in 2011, the five-star St Pancras Renaissance Hotel occupies the lower floors of the former Midland Grand Hotel – once dubbed London's most romantic building – which was designed by Sir George Gilbert Scott and restored for an eye-watering £150+ million. Now featuring 245 guest rooms, it's once again one of London's most iconic destinations with glorious Gothic Revival metalwork, gold leaf ceilings, hand-stencilled wall designs and grand staircase, as dazzling as the day the original Midland opened in 1873.

The old ticket hall, with dark-panelled walls and soaring church-like windows, is now a bar, while the hotel's restaurant (the original grand restaurant space) is appropriately named The Gilbert Scott and run by celebrated chef Marcus Wareing.

St Pancras Renaissance Hotel, Euston Road, NW1 2AR (020-7841 3540; www. stpancrasrenaissance.co.uk; King's X/St Pancras tube; £££-££££).

San Domenico House

Occupying a pair of Victorian red-brick townhouses built in 1887, San Domenico House is a luxury boutique hotel located just steps away from Sloane Square in the heart of vibrant Chelsea. The original house (29 Draycott Place) has seen many changes over its lifetime, from stately family home to separate apartments in the '70s and '80s, until being lovingly restored and redeveloped in 1991 as a luxury boutique hotel, the Sloane Hotel, by interior designer Sue Rogers (and later extended to include the house next door).

Owned since 2005 by the Italian Melpignano family, whose portfolio includes some equally lovely hotels in Puglia, San Domenico is the glossy Italian equivalent of the English country house look at its most florid – all gilt and silk, urns and cherubs – offering a taste of la dolce vita in west London.

Acclaimed as one London's finest boutique hotels, the house has 15 luxurious air-conditioned rooms featuring antique furniture and plush fabrics, with en-suite marble bathrooms, flat-screen TVs, minibars and free wi-fi. Other amenities

include a drawing room (the perfect setting for afternoon tea), business centre and fitness room, plus a 'secret' roof terrace where you can enjoy cocktails and light Italian dishes.

San Domenico House, 29-31 Draycott Pl, SW3 2SH (020-7581 5757; www.sandomenicohouse. com; Sloane Sq tube; £££).

Town Hall Hotel

Once Bethnal Green's main council building and now a luxurious five-star hotel, this beautiful Edwardian structure dates from 1910. It was renovated in 1937 with splendid Art Deco interiors and again in 2007, after which it became the Town Hall

Hotel. The award-winning building combines architectural splendour with cutting-edge design, creating a unique designer hotel that fuses the best of old and new.

The 98 rooms – including 88 spectacular suites – are deliciously inviting, featuring vintage furniture and sheepskin rugs, barista-quality coffee machines, luxury toiletries, an entertainment centre and free wi-fi. The hotel is also home to the excellent Typing Room restaurant, Corner Room bistro and Peg + Patriot cocktail bar.

Town Hall Hotel, Patriot Sq, Bethnal Gn, E2 9NF (020-7871 0460; http://townhallhotel.com; Bethnal Gn tube; ££).

W London

Located in the heart of Leicester Square, W Hotel is a trendy US import with an ultra-modern wrap-around translucent glass façade and décor more befitting a nightclub; disco balls in reception, padded walls, groovy furniture and music from hidden speakers, while public areas are infused with purple and gold neon light. The 192 rooms – classified as Fantastic, Spectacular, Fabulous and Cool (no false modesty here!) – and suites feature funky contemporary interiors, mood lighting, floor-to-ceiling windows, custom beds and flat-screen TVs. The Screening Suite has its own private cinema and steam room!

There's also a sleek cocktail lounge, a south-east Asian inspired restaurant (Spice Market) and a chic nightclub (Room 913), plus a 24-hour gym and luxury spa.

W Hotel, 10 Wardour St, W1D 6QF (020-7758 1000; www.wlondon.co.uk; Leicester Sq tube; £££-££££).

Zetter Townhouse

Zetter Townhouse is a fabulous boutique luxury hotel occupying a Georgian townhouse in Clerkenwell, just a few minutes from the City and West End (there's a sister hotel in Marylebone). The hotel is a beguiling Aladdin's cave, bursting with character, colour and invention, a refreshing oasis in the bland world of corporate hotels. The décor is inviting, sumptuous and quirky, the hotel lounge and bar positively crammed with curiosities, ephemera,

portraits, photos, statues, urns, large comfy wingback chairs and even a stuffed cat in a frock! The end result resembles a cross between an antiques shop, an intimate gentlemen's club and the front parlour of an eccentric maiden aunt.

The 13 rooms (including two suites and an apartment) range from the small but perfectly formed Club to spacious Deluxe rooms with king-size beds, while the suites have freestanding baths and enough room to swing several cats. All mod cons (free wi-fi) and then some, including hot-water bottles and slippers.

The hotel's vaunted cocktail lounge serves cocktails to die for (by Tony Conigliaro of 69 Colebrooke Row – see page 10), plus tasty bar snacks from Bruno Loubet (such as courgette crisps, British charcuterie and sherry trifle), while the basement has a games room with 3D TV, table tennis – and a glimpse of a 16th-century priory wall.

Zetter Townhouse, 49-50 St John's Sq, EC1V 4JJ (020-7324 4444; www.thezettertownhouse.com; Farringdon tube; £££).

8.
Markets

No shopper should visit London without taking in one of its profusion of colourful, lively markets. These range from the behemoths of Borough and Portobello to the authentic neighbourhood vibe of Brixton and Hackney, from the bustling weekend honeypots of Brick Lane and Camden to the more sedate charms of Greenwich and Marylebone.

Markets are a wonderful hunting ground for savvy shoppers, whether you're after cabbages or clothes, handicrafts or household goods, artisan bread or antiques; but they're more than just a retail experience: London's markets are fun as well. Visiting one is a great way to get under the city's skin and see how Londoners trade – just as they have done for centuries – and few things makes you feel more at home than finding and haggling for a bargain.

London's markets also keep you one step ahead of the pack. Independent traders and passionate local communities are at the heart of the capital's market scene, and it's where you'll encounter many of today's budding entrepreneurs, particularly when it comes to food. Many of London's foodie icons got their break on a market stall, be they butchers, bakers or coffee roasters, and today's stallholders are tomorrow's high street stars. No surprise then that markets are excellent places for great value, high quality and amazingly varied street food.

Borough Market

Borough Market in Southwark was first recorded in 1276, although some claim a market has existed in the area since the 11th century and possibly much earlier. Despite changing locations a number of times, and even being temporarily abolished in the 18th century, the market has thrived. Today it's the largest wholesale and retail artisan food market in London, selling a huge variety of produce sourced from throughout Britain and around the globe. It's run by a charitable trust and is the only fully independent market in London.

Since its renaissance as a retail market in the early 21st century – it still operates as a wholesale market from 2-8am on weekdays – Borough Market has become a Mecca for those who care about the quality and provenance of the food they cook, sell or eat, including chefs, restaurateurs, gourmets, foodies and keen amateur cooks.

It seems that anyone who's anyone in London's artisan food world has an outlet at Borough Market, including Artisan du Chocolat, Ginger Pig, Konditor & Cook, Monmouth Coffee and Neal's Yard Dairy. If anywhere in the capital illustrates Britain's newfound love of good food, it's Borough Market.

Borough Market, 8 Southwark St, SE1 1TL (020-7407 1002; www.boroughmarket.org.uk; London Br rail/tube; retail market, Wed-Thu 10am-5pm, Fri 10am-6pm, Sat 8am-5pm, closed Sun).

Brick Lane Market

Brick Lane in Tower Hamlets got its name in the 15th century when it was the home of brick and tile manufacturers, although it later became a centre for the brewing industry. Today, it's a disorganised, artistic, multicultural melting pot, and its weekend markets attract hordes of (mostly young) people in search of second-hand furniture, household goods, records and CDs, cheap antiques, vintage clothing, jewellery, arts and crafts, books, general bric-a-brac and food.

Dating back to the 18th century, the market is pure East End, chaotic and haphazard – somewhere between a treasure trove and a junk heap – with a surprise around every corner.

Brick Lane Market, The Old Truman Brewery, Brick Lane, E1 (020-7770 6028; www. backyardmarket.co.uk, www.boilerhouse-foodhall.co.uk, www.sundayupmarket.co.uk, www.visitbricklane.org; Aldgate E or Shoreditch High St tube; Sat 11am-6pm, Sun 10am-5pm).

Brixton Market

Actually a number of markets thrown together in a gloriously random manner, Brixton Market comprises a vibrant street market and three elegant covered arcades: Reliance Arcade, Market Row and Granville Arcade (now rebranded 'Brixton Village' and packed with culinary treats), which are open daily. A more recent addition is Brixton Station Road, hosting both a food market on Fridays and a Sunday farmers' market.

The market has a bustling atmosphere that you won't find elsewhere in London; whereas many markets are interesting to wander around and browse the wares on offer, Brixton Market is a 'real' market selling a wide choice of world produce at modest prices with minimum frills.

Brixton Market, Electric Ave, Pope's Rd and Brixton Station Rd, SW9 (020-7926 2530; http://brixtonmarket.net; Brixton tube; see website for times).

Broadway & Netil Markets

Broadway and Netil Markets are Saturday markets in East London, where Broadway Market – running from London Fields south to Regent's Canal – has been welcoming shoppers since the 1890s. A Saturday food market was launched in 2004 and now boasts over 100 stalls selling artisan foods, street food and drinks, while

cafés, restaurants, pubs and myriad independent shops line the streets. The market is also popular for its vintage and designer togs, bric-a-brac, books, flowers and crafts.

Neighbouring Netil Market – an altogether more sedate affair – is located on Westgate Street, where you'll find more food stalls plus vintage homeware, jewellery designers, illustrators, original artwork, vintage clothing, accessories and more.

Broadway Market, E8 4QJ (www. broadwaymarket.co.uk; London Fields rail; Sat 9am-5pm): Netil Market, 13-23 Westgate St, E8 3RL (http://netilmarket.tumblr.com; Sat 11am-6pm).

Cabbages & Frocks

The delightfully named Cabbages & Frocks market is held on Saturdays in the cobbled yard of St Marylebone Parish Church (off Marylebone High Street) in Marylebone Village. It's one of London's loveliest neighbourhoods with a wealth of interesting independent shops, cafés and restaurants.

Here you can buy delicious artisan and organic foods – including olive oils, balsamic syrup and vinegars, divine cupcakes, fine breads, olives, cheeses, Argentinian steak sandwiches, hog roast, Japanese delicacies, hot chocolate, organic crepes and galettes, and much more. There are also handicrafts from local designers and cottage industries, including retro and vintage clothing (and children's clothes), homeware, hand-blown glass and jewellery.

Cabbages & Frocks Market, St Marylebone Parish Church Grounds, Marylebone High St, W1U 5BA (020-7794 1636; www. cabbagesandfrocks.co.uk; Baker St tube; Sat 11am-5pm).

Camden Market

Created as an arts and crafts market in the '70s, Camden Market (or markets) is one of the city's coolest destinations for trendy Londoners and visitors. The market is comprised of several adjoining markets in Camden Town near Camden Lock (also called Hampstead Road Lock) on Regent's Canal, collectively called 'Camden Market' or 'Camden Lock'. People flock here to buy an eclectic jumble of bric-a-brac, antiques and collectables, retro and vintage fashion,

ethnic art, rugs and kilims, jewellery, furniture, music and food (especially street food). One of London's most popular and largest markets, it's busiest at weekends when it attracts up to 150,000 bargain hunters.

Camden Lock Market, established in 1974, was the original craft market but now offers a much wider range of goods, while the ever popular Camden Stables Market is the centre of the alternative fashion scene. The market is the creative and cultural heart of London, featuring some of the city's best designers, artists and independent vendors, as well as great food and drink. The West Yard hosts the Global Kitchen (street food heaven) − which wafts its heady aroma of spices across the canal-side terraces − home to some of the city's most exciting street food vendors.

Camden Lock Market, Chalk Farm Rd, NW1 8AF (020-7485 7963; www.camdenmarket.com; Chalk Farm/Camden Town tube; daily 10am-6pm).

Camden Passage Antiques Market

Visiting Camden Passage – an 18th-century cobblestoned pedestrian alley running along the backs of houses on Upper Street in Islington – is like stepping back in time. On Wednesdays and

Saturdays you'll find a variety of stalls selling an eclectic mix of antiques and collectibles – vintage clothes, handbags, jewellery, silver, porcelain, glass and assorted bric-a-brac – surrounded by a range of elegant Georgian antiques shops, pubs, cafés and restaurants.

Whether you're a dealer, interior designer, collector or just a curious browser, you'll find Camden Passage antiques market interesting (not to be confused with Camden Market – see page 129).

Camden Passage Antiques Market, Camden Passage, N1 8EA (www.camdenpassageislington.co.uk; Angel tube; See website for opening hours).

Columbia Road Flower Market

Columbia Road Flower Market is a colourful street market in East London – the city's only dedicated flower market – which grew out of a 19th-century food market. On Sundays the street is transformed into an oasis of foliage and flowers – everything from bedding plants to 10-foot banana trees. Traders, many of whom are also growers and second or third generation, offer a wide range of plants, bedding plants, shrubs, bulbs and freshly cut flowers at competitive prices (even cheaper near closing time).

Columbia Road offers much more than just a flower market and encompasses over 50 independent shops plus a wealth of pubs, cafés and restaurants.

Columbia Road Flower Market, Columbia Rd, E2 7RG (020-7613 0876; www.columbiaroad.info; Hoxton rail; Sun 8am-3pm).

Covent Garden Market

The first Covent Garden market goes back to 1654, although the current market buildings date from the 19th and early 20th centuries. It was previously the home of London's famous fruit, veg and flower market, which moved to Nine Elms in 1974, becoming the New Covent Garden Market (www.newcoventgardenmarket.com). Since then the buildings have been occupied by a number of miscellaneous markets and have become a popular local and tourist attraction. The colonnaded Piazza building houses the Apple Market − with stalls selling British-made souvenirs, fashion, jewellery, artworks, beauty products, collectables and gifts, plus specialty shops, boutiques and cafés − while the East Colonnade offers similar wares, including handmade soap, jewellery, handbags, hand-knitted children's clothing, a magician's stall, sweets, artwork and homewares.

The South Piazza is home to the Jubilee Market (1904), which hosts a Monday antiques market starting from 5am; from

Tuesday to Friday there are stalls selling household goods, clothing, food and gifts; while at weekends it's devoted to arts and crafts, with over 200 artisans selling everything from candles to jewellery, paintings to clocks and calligraphy. This London institution may appear too touristy and crowded to provide a characterful retail experience, but it's good fun and you never know what you might find.

Covent Garden, Southampton St, WC2E 8BE (www.coventgardenlondonuk.com/markets; Covent Gdn tube; Jubilee Market, Mon 5am-5pm, Tue-Fri 10.30am-7pm, Sat-Sun 10am-6pm; Apple Market, Mon 9am-7pm, Tue-Sun 10.30am-7pm).

Greenwich Market

Greenwich has hosted a market since the 14th century, although the present one dates from 1700, and is set in a courtyard of elegant Georgian buildings. The market is actually made up of three markets: the Antiques and Crafts Market, the Village Market and the Central Market. Regarded by many as London's best covered market, it has up to 40 stalls offering antiques and collectables on Mon-Tue and Thu-Fri, and art, craft and design (including fashion and jewellery) on Wed and Fri-Sun.

Greenwich Market also dishes up delicious street food, the menu changing daily, from Thai noodles and Chinese dim sum to Punjabi lamb rogan josh, Israeli falafel to Japanese sushi and Spanish tapas.

Greenwich Market, Greenwich Mkt, SE10 9HZ (020-8269 5096; www.greenwichmarketlondon. com; Cutty Sark DLR; see website for days & times).

Leadenhall Market

Dating back to the 14th century, Leadenhall Market is a restored Victorian covered market selling traditional game, poultry, fish, meat and 'designer' items. The beautiful ornate wrought iron and glass building (painted green, maroon and cream) you see today was designed by Sir Horace Jones in 1881 and is a popular tourist attraction.

Leadenhall Market sells some of the finest food in the City including fresh meat and cheese and delicacies from around the world, and has a variety of other vendors including a florist, a chocolate shop, a pen shop and fashion boutiques, plus a number of restaurants, pubs (try the Lamb Tavern) and wine bars.

Leadenhall Market, Gracechurch St, EC3V 1LT (020-7332 1523; www.cityoflondon.gov.uk/ things-to-do/leadenhall-market; Bank tube; Mon-Fri 10am-6pm, closed Sat-Sun).

Leather Lane Market

One of London's lesser-known but oldest and most interesting markets, Leather Lane Market in the City can trace its history back some 400 years. The lunchtime market sells a bit of everything from fruit and vegetables to DVDs and mobile phones, clothing and footwear to flowers and travel accessories, all at bargain prices.

The market also offers a wealth of street food from a host of food stalls and cafés, from falafel wraps and burritos to hog roasts and jacket potatoes, Italian delis to curry kiosks – and not a McDonalds or Starbucks in sight (but there is Prufrock Coffee).

Leather Lane Market, Leather Ln, EC1N 7TJ (www.leatherlanestars.wordpress.com/the-market; Chancery Ln or Farringdon tube; Mon-Fri 10am-2pm, closed Sat-Sun).

Maltby Street/ Ropewalk Market

Maltby Street in Bermondsey is one of London's newest foodie destinations, where the indie trader spirit thrives. The area between Maltby Street and Millstream Road and the nearby Ropewalk hosts a lively, informal weekend street market (known variously as Maltby Street Market or Ropewalk Market), with a combination of railway arch shops, open stalls, pop-up bars and eateries. It's a more laidback and relaxed affair than nearby Borough Market (see page 126) and has a burgeoning reputation among chefs and foodies.

At weekends the stalls and tables groan under the weight of cupcakes and brownies, seafood and charcuterie, gourmet gelato and oven-fresh bread, and a profusion of fruit and vegetables.

Maltby Street Market, Ropewalk/Maltby St, SE1 3PA (www.timeout.com/london/shopping/maltby-street-se1; Bermondsey tube; Sat 9am-4pm, Sun 11am-4pm).

Partridges Food Market

West London's most popular food market, Partridges (named after a nearby food emporium) began life in 2005 and has grown rapidly in popularity ever since, attracting an average of 70 traders every Saturday (there's a waiting list). Held on Duke of York Square, close to Sloane Square tube station, the market offers a wide range of produce including free-range meats; patisserie, pastries and cakes; organic juices and produce; artisan bread and cheese; fish and seafood; homemade pies; specialist coffees and teas; and a wide range of international specialities and street food.

See the website for a list of traders.

Partridges Food Market, Duke of York Sq, SW3 4LY (020-7730 0651; www.partridges.co.uk/foodmarket; Sloane Sq tube; Sat 10am-4pm).

Petticoat Lane Market

A famous Sunday market operating since the 1750s, Petticoat Lane was named after the petticoats and lace sold there by the Huguenots who came to London from France in the 17th century. The street was renamed Middlesex Street in the 19th century by prudish Victorians who wanted to avoid references to women's underwear, but the original name has stuck.

It's one of London's largest markets with over 1,000 stalls on a Sunday spread over two streets, specialising in new goods ranging from clothing (particularly leatherware) and shoes to kitchenalia and household goods. It remains London's biggest street jumble sale and for bargain hunters – haggling essential – it's the original and the best.

Petticoat Lane Market, Middlesex St, E1 7JF (Aldgate/Aldgate East/Liverpool St tube; Sun 9am-2pm).

Portobello Road

London's largest and most popular market, Portobello Road has been operating for over 150 years, and although it's most famous for its Saturday antiques market, there's much more to it than that. It's several markets rolled into one and includes Portobello Green Market (selling antiques, fashion, jewellery, cakes, food, books, etc., Fri-Sun) and Golborne Road Market (fruit and veg, street food, bric-a-brac, second-hand and household goods, Mon-Fri), in addition to the famous antiques market (the world's largest) on Saturdays, when over 1,000 dealers set up their stalls between Chepstow Villas and Elgin Crescent.

Portobello Green Market is London's leading vintage, retro and boutique fashion market with up to 800 stalls. The market operates from Friday to Sunday under the Westway flyover on Portobello Road offering mainly retro and vintage fashion and accessories (plus collectables) on Fridays; designer clothes, accessories and jewellery on Saturdays; and bric-a-brac, vintage clothes, books, CDs and records, etc. on Sundays.

Head further north for Golborne Road, which hosts one of London's best fruit and veg markets (Mon-Wed) where Londoners flock from miles around to buy their produce, alongside stalls selling knick-knacks, household goods, clothing, furniture, etc. There's also a wide variety of specialist food stalls on most days, particularly on Fridays and Saturdays, including plenty of street food stalls.

Portobello Road Market, Portobello Rd, W11 (www.portobelloroad.co.uk, http:// portobellofashionmarket.com and http:// shopportobello.co.uk; Notting Hill Gate/ Ladbroke Grove tube; Mon-Wed 9am-6pm, Thu 9am-1pm, Fri 9am-7pm, Sat 9am-7pm, Sun – Green Market – 9am-7pm).

9.

Museums & Galleries

London is one of the world's great centres for art and culture – many claim it's the art capital of the world – with more popular museums and galleries than any other city; some 250, excluding commercial galleries. It's also home to seven of the world's top 50 most-visited museums and art galleries, beating rival cities such as New York and Paris.

The London art scene is a lot like the city itself – vast, vibrant, diverse and in a constant state of flux – a cornucopia of traditional and cutting edge, majestic and mundane, world-class and run-of-the-mill, bizarre and brilliant. From Old Masters to street art, London has it all in spades.

Every visitor wants to see the world-class national collections, such as the British Museum and National Gallery, but once you've explored the Egyptian galleries and admired Van Gogh's *Sunflowers*, what next? Then it's time to seek out the city's smaller but equally captivating collections, such as the Wallace Collection and the Dulwich Picture Gallery; visit absorbing 'specialist' museums like Sir John Soane's eclectic house of treasures and the fascinating Horniman; and see controversial, thought-provoking (even shocking) modern art at the Saatchi Gallery and Tate Modern.

London has something for everyone and the wonderful thing about the majority of museums and galleries featured here is that entrance is free!

British Museum

The British Museum is a London landmark and the city's most popular museum, attracting over 7 million visitors annually. Much loved for its mummies and marbles, it provides an almost overwhelming smorgasbord of human history and culture stretching across centuries and continents – a permanent collection of some 8 million objects housed in almost 100 galleries – although only around 1 per cent is on show at any one time.

The Museum grew from the private collection of curiosities bequeathed to George II by physician and scientist Sir Hans Sloane (1660-1753). Sloane's collection comprised around 71,000 objects including books, manuscripts, natural history specimens and antiquities. The museum was established by Act of Parliament in 1753 and opened in 1759 in

Montagu House in Bloomsbury, on the site of the current building. It was the first national public museum in the world, and set a precedent by offering free entry to 'all studious and curious persons'.

The magnificent building you see today was designed by Sir Robert Smirke and completed in 1852. The circular Reading Room opened in 1857 and housed much of the British Library until it moved to St Pancras in 1997, making way for the Great Court; Norman Foster's spectacular glass structure opened in 2000 and is the largest covered public square in Europe. The most recent addition is the World Conservation and Exhibition Centre, which opened in 2014.

British Museum, Great Russell St, WC1B 3DG (020-7323 8299; www.britishmuseum.org; Tottenham Court Rd tube; daily 10am-5.30pm, Fri 8.30pm; free).

Courtauld Gallery

Situated at the heart of the Courtauld Institute of Art, a world leader in the study of art history and conservation, the Courtauld Gallery contains a gem of an art collection created by bequests made by Samuel Courtauld (1876-1947) in the '30s and '40s.

The gallery is located in spectacular Somerset House (1776), and houses a celebrated collection of over 530 paintings and 26,000

Self-portrait, Vincent van Gogh

drawings and prints, ranging from the early Renaissance to modernist works of the 20th century. It includes a splendid array of Gothic and medieval paintings, plus Renaissance masterpieces by artists such as Cranach and Brueghel. Baroque highlights include iconic paintings by Rubens, while Post-Impressionist works include Van Gogh's iconic *Self-portrait with Bandaged Ear*.

Courtauld Gallery, Somerset House, Strand, WC2R 0RN (020-7848 2526; www.courtauld. ac.uk; Temple tube; daily 10am-6pm; adults £7, concessions £6, under 18s free).

Dulwich Picture Gallery

Designed by Sir John Soane (1753-1837) and opened in 1817, the beautiful Dulwich Picture Gallery was England's first purpose-built public art gallery, and its design – flooded with natural light – has proved highly influential in the way we view art. The collection itself was mainly bequeathed by art dealers Francis Bourgeois and Noel Deschamps, and was originally assembled between 1790 and 1795 for the King of Poland.

The gallery houses one of the world's most important collections of European 17th/18th-century Old Masters and includes works by Canaletto, Constable, Gainsborough, Hogarth, Landseer, Murillo, Poussin, Raphael, Rembrandt, Reynolds, Rubens and Van Dyck.

Dulwich Picture Gallery, Gallery Rd, Dulwich, SE21 7AD (020-8693 5254; www. dulwichpicturegallery.org.uk; W or N Dulwich rail; Tue-Sun 10am-5pm, closed Mon; £7 adults, £6 seniors, free for unemployed, students and children under 18).

Guildhall Art Gallery

Established in 1886, as 'a collection of art treasures worthy of the capital city', the Guildhall Art Gallery houses the collection of the City of London and displays around 250 works of art at any one time (from a total collection of some 4,500), which have been amassed since the 17th century. It contains paintings from 1670 to the present day, including works by Constable, Rossetti, Landseer and Millais; the centrepiece of the largest gallery is John Singleton Copley's huge painting *The Defeat of the Floating Batteries of Gibraltar*.

In the basement of the gallery are the remains of a Roman amphitheatre (AD70) discovered during an archaeological dig in preparation for building the current gallery.

Guildhall Art Gallery, Guildhall Yd (off Gresham St), EC2V 5AE (020-7332 3700; www. cityoflondon.gov.uk/thingstodo; Bank tube; Mon-Sat 10am-5pm, Sun noon-4pm; free).

Horniman Museum

Opened in 1901 in a lovely Arts and Crafts/Art Nouveau-style building designed by Charles Harrison Townsend, the Horniman Museum was founded by the Victorian tea trader Frederick John Horniman (1835-1906). It houses his superb collection of cultural artefacts, ethnography, natural history and musical instruments, totalling over 350,000 objects – some collected personally on his travels (although he didn't leave Britain until he was 60), but most accumulated by his tea merchants.

The museum is noted for its unique design, including a modern aquarium in the basement, and is set in 16 acres of award-winning, beautifully maintained gardens, which include a Grade II listed conservatory, bandstand, animal enclosure, nature trail, ornamental garden, shop and café.

Horniman Museum, 100 London Rd, Forest Hill, SE23 3PQ (020-8699 1872; www.horniman.ac.uk; Forest Hill rail; daily 10.30am-5.30pm; free).

Imperial War Museum London

Founded in 1917, the Imperial War Museum is the world's leading authority on conflict and its impact, focusing on Britain, its former Empire and the Commonwealth, from the First World War to the present day. The museum illustrates and records all aspects of modern warfare, whether allied or enemy, service or civilian, military or political,

social or cultural. The collections include archives of personal and official documents, photography, film and video material, and oral history recordings; an extensive library; a large art collection; and examples of military vehicles and aircraft, equipment and other artefacts.

Following a £40 million transformation, a suite of permanent new galleries was opened in 2014 to mark the centenary of the First World War.

Imperial War Museum London, Lambeth Rd, SE1 6HZ (020-7416 5000; www.iwm.org.uk/visits/iwm-london; Lambeth N tube; daily 10am-6pm; free).

Museum of London

The Museum of London is the largest urban history museum in the world and although it's primarily concerned with the social history of London, it also maintains its archaeological interests. The museum is an amalgamation of two earlier museums: the Guildhall Museum, founded in 1826, and the London Museum, founded in 1912. Its nine permanent galleries tell the story of the capital from prehistory to today, and feature everything from Roman mosaics to the copper cauldron that held the flame at the 2012 London Olympics.

The museum underwent a £20m redesign in 2010, increasing the space by a quarter. In 2015 it was announced that it would be moving to a new site in Smithfield Market.

Museum of London, 150 London Wall, EC2Y 5HN (020-7001 9844; www.museumoflondon.org.uk/london-wall; Barbican tube; daily 10am-6pm; free).

Lord Mayor of London's State Coach

National Gallery

One of the finest collections of Western European art, the National Gallery is the fifth most-visited art museum in the world with almost 6 million visitors annually and is a must-see for anyone interested in art. It boasts over 2,300 works of art, dating from the 13th century to 1900 – from Botticelli's *Venus and Mars* to Constable's *The Hay Wain*. The building was designed by William Wilkins and opened in 1838, and has been continually expanded over the years as the collection has grown, most recently with the addition of the Sainsbury Wing, the Postmodernist extension that opened in 1991.

The National Gallery's paintings are grouped chronologically and displayed in four wings. The Sainsbury Wing hosts medieval and early works, while the 16th-century Renaissance paintings are housed in the West Wing. The North Wing to the rear is home to 17th-century works and the East Wing contains 18th- and 19th-century

paintings, including the British School. The Gallery's map is colour-coded and easy to navigate, and the website version is interactive so you can see at a glance which paintings are in which room.

It's a museum for contemplation rather than interaction, and one that deserves to be dipped into time and again.

National Gallery, Trafalgar Sq, WC2N 5DN (020-7747 2885; www.nationalgallery.org.uk; Charing Cross tube/rail; daily 10am-6pm, 9pm Fridays; free).

National Maritime Museum

Officially opened in 1937, the National Maritime Museum is the largest museum of its kind in the world. The historic buildings (mostly Grade I listed) form part of the Maritime Greenwich World Heritage Site and incorporate the Royal Observatory and the 17th-century Queen's House.

The museum's collection comprises some 2.5 million items on the history of Britain at sea, from tea

The Bretagne, Jules Achille Noël

chests and cannonballs to the coat Nelson wore at the Battle of Trafalgar. Categories include maritime art (both British and 17th-century Dutch); cartography; manuscripts; model ships; scientific and navigational instruments, and instruments for time-keeping and astronomy (based at the Royal Observatory). The museum also houses the world's largest maritime historical reference library (100,000 volumes).

National Maritime Museum, Romney Road, Greenwich, SE10 9NF (020-8858 4422; www.rmg. co.uk/national-maritime-museum; Cutty Sark DLR; daily 10am-5pm; free).

National Portrait Gallery

Founded by Philip Henry Stanhope and established in 1856, the National Portrait Gallery was the first of its kind in the world. The gallery building was designed by architect Ewan Christian in rather fanciful Florentine style, and opened to the public

in 1896; it has been extended twice, in 1933 when the Duveen Wing was opened and in 2000 when the Ondaatje Wing was added.

Whether you're seeking artistic inspiration or simply like looking at famous faces, you'll find plenty to entertain you in

King Henry VIII

the NPG. The unique collection of portraits shows famous and influential British people from the last 500 years – from Henry VIII to Winston Churchill – captured in paintings, sculpture, drawings and photography. The collection includes over 300,000 images, including some 11,000 portraits.

National Portrait Gallery, St Martin's Pl, WC2H 0HE (020-7306 0055; www.npg.org.uk; Leicester Sq tube; daily 10am-6pm, 9pm Thu-Fri; free).

Natural History Museum

From dinosaurs to diamonds, the Natural History Museum is one of London's most enthralling destinations and is especially popular with children. Covering all aspects of life and earth sciences, it doesn't just preserve the past but also seeks to preserve our planet by providing a hub for research and education.

The museum began as a collection of specimens donated to the nation by Sir Hans Sloane in 1753 and didn't get its own home until 1881. Designed by Alfred Waterhouse, the museum building is one of the most architecturally pleasing in Britain: a Romanesque confection clad in terracotta tiles. The vast collection contains some 70 million items grouped in five main collections – botany, entomology, mineralogy, palaeontology and zoology – spread over five floors.

Natural History Museum, Cromwell Rd, SW7 5BD (020-7942 5000; www.nhm.ac.uk; S Kensington tube; daily 10am-5.50pm; free).

Royal Academy of Arts

Founded in 1768 and located in Burlington House – one of London's finest Palladian buildings – the Royal Academy of Arts (RA for short) is an independent institution run by eminent artists to promote the creation and appreciation of visual arts. The highlight of the Academy's year is its annual Summer Exhibition (June to August), which attracts thousands of applications from both amateur and professional artists.

The RA also holds regular temporary loan presentations that elevate its international prestige and importance, which have included such crowd pleasers as The Real Van Gogh: The Artist and His Letters (2010), David Hockney RA: A Bigger Picture (2012) and Ai Weiwei (2015).

Royal Academy of Arts, Burlington House, Piccadilly, W1J 0BD (020-7300 8000; www. royalacademy.org.uk; Green Pk tube; daily 10am-6pm, 10pm Fri; see website for exhibition prices and free tours).

Saatchi Gallery

Civilzation, Bai Yiluo

The brainchild of advertising guru Charles Saatchi, who first opened his gallery in 1985 to exhibit his private collection of contemporary art, the Saatchi Gallery has been housed in the splendid Duke of York's HQ (Grade II* listed) in Chelsea since 2008. It's been praised as one of 'the most beautiful art spaces in London' with some 70,000ft² (6,500m²) of exhibition space.

The gallery is a major influence on art in Britain and has a history of media controversy with extremes of critical reaction. Love it or hate it, the Saatchi never fails to provoke a reaction and has gone from strength to strength. It's one of London's most popular galleries, attracting over 1.5 million visitors annually.

Saatchi Gallery, Duke of York's HQ, King's Rd, SW3 4RY (020-7811 3070; www.saatchi-gallery. co.uk; Sloane Sq tube; daily 10am-6pm, but check it's open before travelling; free).

Science Museum

Created in the wake of the Great Exhibition of 1851 as part of the South Kensington Museum, the Science Museum didn't become an independent entity until 1909. The current building opened in 1928 and was little changed until 2000, when the Welcome Wing opened as a platform for contemporary science and technology.

Today, the museum provides a seamless link from before the Industrial Revolution to the 21st century and beyond. It has assembled a priceless collection of over 300,000 items, from steam engines to space modules, and visiting it feels like taking a ride on a machine that's in perpetual motion, with exhibits (on seven floors) encompassing a blend of static displays and hands-on interactives. Fascinating for children of all ages.

Science Museum, Exhibition Rd, SW7 2DD (020-7942 4000; www.sciencemuseum.org.uk; S Kensington tube; daily 10am-6pm; free).

Sir John Soane's Museum

Sir John Soane (1753-1837) was a bricklayer's son who became one of Britain's greatest architects, noted for his designs for the Bank of England and the Dulwich Picture Gallery (see page 139). The museum is located in his former home, which he designed both to live in and to house his antiquities and works of art.

Soane amassed a huge collection of fascinating objects and artworks including Roman cremation urns, the Egyptian sarcophagus of Seti I and pieces from the classical, medieval, Renaissance and Oriental periods, including furniture, timepieces, stained glass, drawings, paintings, sculptures, jewellery and architectural models. Paintings include significant works by Canaletto, Piranesi, Reynolds, Turner and Hogarth, including all eight of Hogarth's *Rake's Progress* series.

Sir John Soane's Museum, 13 Lincoln's Inn Fields, WC2A 3BP (020-7405 2107; www.soane. org; Holborn tube; Tue-Sat 10am-5pm, closed Sun-Mon; free).

Tate Britain

The original Tate gallery opened in 1897 to provide a dedicated home for British art and nowadays attracts over 1.5 million art lovers annually. A major rebranding in 2000 saw its modern art moved down the River Thames to Tate Modern at Bankside (see below) while Tate Britain, as it's now known, majors in historic and contemporary art.

The gallery's permanent collection dates from 1500 to the present day, and is one of the most comprehensive of its kind in the world. It includes a priceless display of works by Turner, as well as Gainsborough, Hogarth, Constable, Stubbs, Bacon, Moore, Hockney and many more. Take time out to visit the Rex Whistler Restaurant and see Whistler's massive mural, *The Expedition in Pursuit of Rare Meats*.

Tate Britain, Millbank, SW1P 4RG (020-7887 8888; www.tate.org.uk; Pimlico/Vauxhall tube; daily 10am-6pm; free).

Tate Modern

The Tate Modern is one of the runaway success stories of the British arts scene. Opened in 2000 to provide a dedicated space in which to display the Tate's burgeoning collection of 20th-century art – from Matisse and Picasso to Warhol and

Damien Hirst – it's the most visited modern art gallery in the world, attracting almost 5 million visitors annually.

Its location in the former Bankside Power Station is as visually arresting as the art inside. Originally designed by Sir Giles Gilbert Scott (also famous for Liverpool Cathedral, Waterloo Bridge, Battersea Power Station and the iconic red telephone box), the building, with its distinctive 325ft central tower, was built in the post-war years and was in service until 1981. The scale and grandeur of the building complements its contents and is the perfect space in which to display

installations and live art, which nowadays are seen as as important as traditional paintings and sculpture. The permanent collections consist of works of international modern and contemporary art dating from 1900 to the current day.

The museum is constantly evolving to meet demand and in 2016 unveiled a new extension (part of a £260 million revamp) called the Switch House, a pyramid-like ten-story tower housing cavernous gallery spaces, enabling 60 per cent more artworks to go on display.

Tate Modern, Bankside, SE1 9TG (020-7887 8888; www.tate.org.uk; Southwark tube; daily 10am-6pm, Fri-Sat 10pm; free).

Autumn, Henri Laurens

Victoria & Albert Museum

The Victoria and Albert Museum (V&A for short) is the world's leading museum of art and design, and its collections include glass and ceramics, textiles and costumes, metalwork and jewellery, domestic items and furniture, along with a wealth of fine art. Its permanent collection numbers over 2.2 million objects, of which around 60,000 are displayed at any one time. Exhibits are divided into five main themes – Asia, Europe, Materials & Techniques, Modern and Exhibitions – displayed in 145 galleries.

The museum was established in 1852, after the Great Exhibition, at the instigation of Prince Albert, who was disappointed that Britain, while excelling in manufacturing, missed out on design prizes. He wanted a museum of applied arts that would inspire and educate people, and was assisted by Henry Cole – inventor of the Christmas card – who became the museum's first director. Five years later the collection moved to its current site and was officially opened by Queen Victoria in June 1857.

Throughout the next four decades, buildings were added and extended and in 1899 work began on a new building by Aston Webb, which provides the museum with its distinctive façade. When Queen Victoria laid the foundation stone on 17th May that year – her last official public appearance – the Victoria and Albert Museum was born.

Victoria & Albert Museum, Cromwell Rd, SW7 2RL (020-7942 2000; www.vam.ac.uk; S Kensington tube; daily 10am-5.45pm, Fri selected galleries until 10pm; free).

Wallace Collection

Located in a handsome 18th-century Georgian house in Manchester Square, the Wallace Collection is a treasure trove of fine and decorative arts dating from the 15th to 19th centuries and spread over 25 galleries. It contains a wealth of French 18th-century paintings, furniture (one of the finest collections of French furniture outside France), Sèvres porcelain, arms and armour, and Old Master paintings.

Laughing Cavalier, Franz Hals

It's mainly the collection of the first four Marquesses of Hertford, particularly the fourth, Richard Seymour-Conway (1800-1870), who left it and the house to his illegitimate son Sir Richard Wallace (1818-1890). Wallace was also an important contributor to the collection, which was bequeathed to the nation by his widow in 1897. It opened to the public in 1900 on condition that no object would ever leave the collection, even for temporary exhibition elsewhere; even today, no works can be stored off-site.

The collection contains around 5,500 objects divided into six curatorial departments: pictures and miniatures; ceramics and glass; sculpture and works of art; arms and armour; Sèvres porcelain; and gold boxes and furniture. The paintings include important works by Canaletto, Delacroix, Fragonard, Gainsborough, Hals (*The Laughing Cavalier*), Landseer, Murillo, Poussin, Rembrandt, Reynolds, Rubens, Titian, Turner, Van Dyck and Velasquez. There's also a world-class collection of arms and armour (European and Oriental), plus bronzes, enamels, glass, majolica, miniatures and sculpture – in short, something to appeal to almost everyone.

Wallace Collection, Hertford House, Manchester Sq, W1U 3BN (020-7563 9500; www. wallacecollection.org; Bond St tube; daily 10am-5pm; free).

10.
Music

From Dingwalls to the Royal Albert Hall, London's live music venues are as legendary as some of the artists who perform there. Whether your taste is for something modern or classical, experimental or traditional, chilled out or head-bangingly loud, you'll find a gig, session or concert somewhere in London that appeals. The range and scale of venues is vast and all musical genres are catered to, be they folk, rock, jazz, hip-hop, pop, rap, R&B, chamber music, orchestral or blues.

From the 100 Club to the Roundhouse, London has long been at the forefront of musical innovation and its vibrant underground music scene means that there are always new artists to discover. It's also home to some world-class orchestras and hosts the world's longest-running music festival, the Promenade Concerts (or Proms).

What makes London unique is the huge number of venues that stage concerts on a daily or weekly basis. This chapter spans the whole breadth of the city's musical hotspots, from vast concert halls and arenas such as the O2 to intimate local joints like Café OTO. It also takes in hip rock venues such as the Brixton Academy, temples to jazz like Ronnie Scott's, and the classical splendour of the Cadogan and Wigmore Halls.

If that's not enough choice, many pubs and bars feature live music, and live performances are a highlight at many nightclubs (see **Chapter 11**).

100 Club

One of London's oldest and most iconic music clubs, the 350-capacity basement 100 Club in Oxford Street has been around since 1942 when it was the Feldman Swing Club. Many musical legends have performed at the Club including Louis Armstrong, Billie Holliday, Muddy Waters, the Who, the Kinks, the Sex Pistols, the Clash and just about every notable Britpop band. It staged the first Northern Soul All-Nighter in the '80s and early shows from Oasis and Suede in the '90s, as well as key shows from artists such as the Horrors, Gallows and Kings of Leon in the 2000s.

It's grungy – the décor hasn't changed since the '70s – but with great atmosphere.

100 Club, 100 Oxford St, W1D 1LL (020-7636 0933; www.the100club.co.uk: Tottenham Court Rd tube; Sun-Fri 7.30-11pm, Sat 7.30pm-1am).

606 Club

An intimate, informal jazz club and restaurant at the 'wrong' end of Chelsea, the 606 Club is owned by Steve Rubie and has been part of London's music scene since 1976. Offering live music seven nights a week – featuring almost exclusively British-based musicians – the 150-capacity 606 caters to a diverse crowd of serious jazz types and partygoers in search of late-night sustenance and sounds.

There's no stand-alone entry fee and bands are funded from a cover charge (which goes entirely to the musicians) that's added to your bill at the end of the night. Alcohol is only served to non-members with a meal. Booking is advisable.

606 Club, 90 Lots Rd, SW10 0QD (020-7352 5953; www.606club.co.uk; Fulham Broadway tube; see website for opening times).

The Barbican Arts Centre

Taking pride of place in the vast 40-acre Barbican Estate, the Barbican Arts Centre is the largest arts venue in Europe. It's noted for its excellence in the performing arts – it has two theatres and a cinema – and for bringing visual art to the public, but also makes a significant contribution to the capital's musical heritage.

Both the London Symphony Orchestra and BBC Symphony Orchestra are based in the Centre's 1,949 seat Barbican Hall, which has excellent acoustics. It also hosts visiting musicians, such as Amsterdam's Royal Concertgebouw Orchestra, concerts by contemporary and experimental musicians, and events like the London Jazz Festival. Just along Silk Street is Milton Court, part of the Guildhall School of Music and Drama, a partner of the Barbican Arts Centre, which has its own 608-seater hall and hosts two associate ensembles: the Academy of Ancient Music and Britten Sinfonia.

Opened in 1982, the Barbican is owned and managed by the City of London Corporation, the third-largest funder of arts in the UK. Its (Grade II listed) Brutalist design is still controversial over 35 years on – it was once voted the ugliest building in London – but what is undisputed is that its calendar plays host to some of the world's greatest musical talent.

The Barbican Arts Centre, Silk St, EC2Y 8BS (020-7638 4141; www.barbican.org.uk/music; Barbican tube).

Brixton Academy

Opened in 1929 as the Astoria cinema, the 5,000-capacity Brixton Academy – officially the O2 Academy Brixton – is one of London's largest non-stadium music venues. It mainly hosts live music – rock, indie, hip-hop and the occasional superstar doing an 'intimate' show – plus club nights, comedy shows and more.

The Academy's design – with its distinctive 140ft dome and Art Deco interior – provides a magnificent backdrop, while sloping floors (at least in the stalls) offer superb views and the vast curved ceiling lends it an electrifying arena-style atmosphere. The iconic stage design is based on Venice's Rialto Bridge and frames Europe's largest fixed stage. Unfortunately the acoustics aren't among the best around, although it has a great atmosphere and, despite its size, feels quite cosy.

The Brixton Academy has played a prominent part in rock history, hosting an incredible line-up of artists over the years and witnessing a wealth of legendary performances. Playing here has become a rite of passage for musicians – the Academy is London's landmark theatre music venue and has witnessed many career-defining headline acts. Amy Winehouse, the Clash, Rhianna, the Sex Pistols, the Smiths, Lady Gaga, Dire Straits, Madonna, the Police, Eric Clapton, Kasabian, Bob Dylan, the Strokes, Blur, Coldplay, UB40 and many more have performed here, and it remains one of the most celebrated rock venues in the UK and worldwide.

Brixton Academy, 211 Stockwell Rd, SW9 9SL (020-7771 3000; www.academymusicgroup.com/ o2academybrixton; Brixton tube).

Bush Hall

Built in 1904 as a dance hall, Bush Hall has had a chequered life, including spells as a soup kitchen, bingo hall, rehearsal space (for the likes of the Who, Adam Faith and Cliff Richard), and a snooker and social club. Restored to its former glory in 2001 by its present owners, it's now an independent music venue.

Ian Skelly/Serpent Power

The exterior is unprepossessing, but step inside the (350-capacity) Hall to discover beautiful Edwardian plasterwork and Austrian lead crystal chandeliers which, coupled with the excellent acoustics, make it an effective and elegant music venue. It's hugely popular for sponsored gigs and for 'secret' shows by major artists – Paul Weller, Adele, Bastille, Ellie Goulding and Suede have all played here in recent years.

Bush Hall, 310 Uxbridge Rd, W12 7LJ (020-8222 6955; www.bushhallmusic.co.uk; Shepherd's Bush Mkt tube).

Cadogan Hall

A former church dating from 1901, with a lovely Byzantine-style exterior and gorgeous Art Deco interior, Cadogan Hall was refurbished and reopened as a concert hall in 2004. It's one of London's most attractive and intimate classical music venues; the sheer walls and steep barrelled roof of the 950-seat auditorium give it great acoustics.

The home of the Royal Philharmonic Orchestra – and a popular choice for many leading touring and international orchestras – Cadogan Hall is also the chosen venue for the world-famous BBC Proms Chamber Music Series. It offers a varied programme of contemporary, jazz, folk and world music events, as well as talks, debates and conferences.

Cadogan Hall, 5 Sloane Ter, SW1X 9DQ (020-7730 4500; www.cadoganhall.com; Sloane Sq tube).

Café OTO

Opened in 2008, Café OTO in Dalston isn't your typical live venue; a café by day with a Persian-inspired menu, in the evening it mutates into a 200-capacity hip music club with avant-garde music, from free jazz to psych rock. Although perhaps best known for hosting free jazz legends such as Peter Brötzmann, Roscoe Mitchell and Evan Parker, OTO's programme is genuinely eclectic. It embraces all manner of world, free-improvised and experimental music, such as Mali's desert blues diva Khaira Arby, minimalist composer Terry Riley and the Sun Ra Arkestra.

The excellent bar stays open until 12.30am and serves a great choice of European and local beers, including ales from Bermondsey's Kernal microbrewery.

Café OTO, 18-22 Ashwin St, E8 3DL (020-7923 1231; www.cafeoto.co.uk; Dalston Junction/ Kingsland rail).

Cecil Sharp House

Maz O'Connor & Simon Jones

A world-class folk arts centre, iconic Cecil Sharp House (built in 1929, Grade II listed and named after the founding father of the folklore revival) is the HQ of the English Folk Dance and Song Society, the national folk arts development organisation for England. The society hosts a variety of concerts, lectures, multimedia events and social dances, plus a comprehensive programme of classes, courses, workshops and talks about dance, music and song.

The Society's diary is packed with barn dances, ceilidhs and the occasional ukulele shenanigan, and this historic venue has hosted performances by some of the biggest names in folk and popular music.

Cecil Sharp House, 2 Regent's Park Rd, NW1 7AY (020-7485 2206; www.cecilsharphouse.org; Camden Town tube).

Dingwalls

Established in 1973, legendary Dingwalls (the name of the building's original owner daubed across an outside wall) is a historic music venue located in Camden Lock. A prominent hang out in the pub rock and punk rock era of the mid to late '70s – the Stranglers, the Clash and Blondie performed and partied there – in more recent years, acts have included established and emerging artists such as the Foo Fighters, Ellie Goulding, the Strokes, Mumford & Sons and White Denim. It's also a popular venue for clandestine shows from big bands.

Nowadays Dingwalls is more comedy club than music venue, although on the right night with the right band, the magic of the old place shines through, reprising the atmospheric powerhouse of yesteryear.

Dingwalls, 11 Middle Yd, Camden Lock, NW1 8AB (020-7428 5929; http://dingwalls.com; Camden Town tube).

The Dublin Castle

There are many, many pubs in London offering live music, but few do it better than the Dublin Castle, a laid-back, family-run pub in Camden that's a legend on the indie scene with gigs seven days a week. Among the many top acts that have performed here are Blur, Madness, the Arctic Monkeys, the Killers, Coldplay and Amy Winehouse (who was a regular). However, you're more likely to see up-and-coming bands – some good, some terrible – with up to four acts booked every night.

There's a dance floor with DJs after gigs from Friday to Sunday, plus a fabulous jukebox in the front bar and cheap drinks. Loud, grungy and grubby, the Dublin Castle is a legend.

Dublin Castle, 94 Parkway, NW1 7AN (020-7485 1773; http://thedublincastle.com; Camden Town tube; Mon-Wed noon-1am, Thu-Sun noon-2am).

Electric Ballroom

Established by Bill Fuller (as the Buffalo Club) in the '30s, the Electric Ballroom is one of the capital's best-loved venues, hosting club nights, live bands, and daytime collectors' fairs and markets at weekends. Over the years the Ballroom (capacity 1,100) has played host to top musical acts such as the Killers, Stereophonics, Paul

McCartney, Frank Zappa, Kaiser Chiefs, U2, Prince, the Clash, the Boomtown Rats, Joy Division, Talking Heads, the Smiths, Madness, Red Hot Chilli Peppers, Public Enemy, Blur, Supergrass, Garbage and many more.

It looks dated now, but is still a really cool place with a great 'rock 'n roll club' atmosphere, super sound system and huge dance floor.

Electric Ballroom, 184 Camden High St, NW1 8QP (020-7485 9006; http://electricballroom. co.uk; Camden Town tube; see website for opening times and gigs).

Eventim Apollo

Arguably London's leading concert venue since the '70s, the Hammersmith Odeon has played host to all the biggest names. Currently called the Eventim Apollo, this Grade II* listed Art Deco building, which originally opened in 1932, is one of the UK's largest and best-preserved theatres. Just about every rocker of note has played here, from Queen and Bruce Springsteen to Iron Maiden and Motorhead, and many have recorded live albums on the Odeon/Apollo stage.

The acoustics are excellent, while the venue is intimate enough (it holds just over 3,600 seated or 5,000 standing) for you to get up close and personal to acts that usually play much bigger arenas, which makes for a tremendous atmosphere.

Eventim Apollo, 45 Queen Caroline St, W6 9QH (020-8563 3800; www.eventimapollo.com; Hammersmith tube).

The Garage

Reckless Love

Opened in 1993, the Garage in Highbury quickly established itself as one of the city's finest club-sized indie and rock venues, and performing here became something of a rite of passage for bands in their early careers. Acts that have played at the Garage include Green Day, Muse, Arctic Monkeys, Franz Ferdinand, Temples, Radiohead, Jagwar Ma, Red Hot Chilli Peppers, Paramore, Oasis, My Chemical Romance, Stereophonics, the Killers, Mumford & Sons and Suede.

Although it has lost some its lustre and is no longer a mainstay of the London club circuit, the Garage remains a great place to watch live gigs. A refurbishment some years ago increased the capacity and improved the sound and atmosphere.

The Garage, 20-22 Highbury Corner, N5 1RD (020-7619 6720; http://thegaragehighbury.com; Highbury & Islington rail).

Islington Assembly Hall

Opened in 1930, Islington Assembly Hall was a popular venue for tea dances and variety shows, but fell into disuse and closed in the '80s. After lying dormant for three decades it was restored and reopened in 2010, retaining many of its original Art Deco features and huge proscenium-arch stage (even the toilets are lovely). It has since become one of the capital's most exciting live music venues, attracting a host of big names and up-and-coming artists.

With an 800 capacity, Islington Assembly Hall is one of the city's best mid-sized venues and a magical place to take in a gig – as a bonus there are lots of terrific pubs, bars and restaurants nearby.

Islington Assembly Hall, Upper St, N1 2UD (020-7527 8900; www.islington.gov.uk/assemblyhall; Essex Rd rail).

Jamboree

Red Sky at Night/Jamboree Collective

One of east London's best live music venues set within the creative melting pot of Cable Street Studios in Limehouse, Jamboree harks back to 1900s vaudeville, Paris in the '30s or a prohibition-era speakeasy. Its programme offers music from across the globe, so you could be greeted with Celtic folk, Costa Rican strings, bluegrass, country classics or travelling swing – every night is unique.

The website says it all: 'Peel back the velvet curtain and step inside a home-made den of world music with devil may care European bohemia, crackled walls and mismatched furniture, raucous evenings, a rag-tag of eccentric characters, flowing absinthe and mad dancing. Order local ale from the charmingly peculiar bar man, possibly wearing a ripped ladies' pinafore with Pat Butcher earrings… and pull up a seat to watch the Mad Hatter's tea party begin.'

Jamboree's atmospheric interior – part bar/club, part junk shop – is a mishmash of quirky items and cast-offs, from antique gramophones to musical instruments, salvaged lampshades to battered Chesterfields, dimly lit by flickering candles and dangling lamps. Bohemian, hip, maybe

a bit rough around the edges, its raucous sounds, eccentric characters and cool cocktails make it one of the city's most original and fun nightspots.

Jamboree, Cable Street Studios, 566 Cable St, E1W 3HB (020-7791 5659; www.jamboreevenue. co.uk; Limehouse DLR; Mon-Thu 7-11pm, Fri-Sat 8-midnight, Sun – see event listings).

O2 Arena

The skyline-grabbing O2 Arena is part of the reinvention of the Millennium Dome which was built to house an exhibition celebrating the turn of the third millennium in 2000. Designed by architect Richard Rogers, the Dome is 365m in diameter and dominates the Greenwich Peninsula in southeast London. It was renamed the O2 in 2005, and redeveloped as an entertainment centre, including an indoor arena – the O2 Arena – a music club, cinema, exhibition space, piazzas, bars and restaurants.

The centrepiece of the redeveloped Dome, the 23,000-capacity O2 Arena is the first purpose-built music venue in London – it's stolen the crown from Wembley Arena – and one of most popular in the world. Host to the biggest names in entertainment – especially those with huge productions requiring an immense space – the O2 has welcomed the Rolling Stones, Justin

Paul McCartney

Timberlake, Miley Cyrus, Tina Turner, Beyonce, AC/DC, Iron Maiden, Metallica, Kings of Leon, Britney Spears, Prince, Katy Perry, Led Zeppelin, Pink Floyd and Robbie Williams, to name just a few.

The O2 Arena also hosts live comedy and TV events, family entertainment such as Disney on Ice and a variety of sports events, including the ATP World Tour tennis finals. Note that it can take a good 20 minutes to exit the Arena, so allow extra time when using public transport.

O2 Arena, Peninsula Sq, SE10 0DX (020-8463 2000; www.theo2.co.uk/do-more-at-the-o2/the-o2-arena; N Greenwich tube).

The Piano Works

Located in a Victorian warehouse in Farringdon, the Piano Works is a live music venue, dance club and bar. What makes it unique – in addition to the venue – is that it's the audience who decide the playlist: the two pianists and accompanying musicians play the crowd's requested repertoire.

Most definitely not an intimate piano bar, the Works is a loud, rollicking saloon with room for 400 revellers and a great party place to come late, stay later still and dance until you drop. The classic bar food is straightforward and matches the drinks (good cocktails) well. The Piano Works is, of course, fairly cheesy – but that's why it's such fun!

The Piano Works, 113-117 Farringdon Rd, EC1R 3BX, entrance on corner of Ray St (020-7278 1966; http://pianoworks.bar; Farringdon tube/ rail; daily 5pm-1am).

Pizza Express Jazz Club

An unlikely combination of pizza joint and jazz club – opened by company founder Peter Boizot in 1969 – the basement Pizza Express Jazz Club in Dean Street is a great place to listen to some cool jazz. It's one of Europe's best modern, mainstream jazz venues, where many of the world's finest jazz musicians have taken to the stage, including Norah Jones, Amy Winehouse, Scott Hamilton, Jamie Cullum and Walter Smith III. Although the biggest stars are rare nowadays, there are still some excellent residencies and emerging talent is encouraged.

With an intimate atmosphere and state-of-the-art sound system, it's a great place to enjoy some cool jazz – and the pizza is really tasty, too.

Pizza Express Jazz Club, 10 Dean St, W1D 3RW (020-7439 4962; www.pizzaexpresslive.com/ jazzlist.aspx; Tottenham Court Rd tube; daily 11am-11pm or later).

Ronnie Scott's

London's most famous jazz club, founded in 1959 by saxophonists Ronnie Scott and Pete King, Ronnie Scott's was inspired by the vibrant New York jazz scene of the '50s. The club was a key player in Soho's jazz explosion in the '60s and '70s, and despite the passing of Scott in 1996 it still retains some of its original electrifying atmosphere.

Today, Ronnie Scott's remains one of the world's most famous jazz clubs, attracting huge audiences practically every night. It's just as popular with performers, who shun the concert halls in favour of Ronnie's cosy ambience. In the early days the club hosted the likes of Sarah Vaughn, Count Basie and Miles Davis – Jimi Hendrix gave his last public performance here in 1970 – and it continues to attract the biggest names in jazz, such as Wynton Marsalis, Cassandra Wilson and Kurt Elling.

With the introduction of the Late Late Show, a relaxed '50s speakeasy vibe, the Wednesday Jazz Jam (a late-night instrumental jazz jam session) and Ronnie's Bar (upstairs at the club) with an eclectic programme of DJ sets and live music (including Latin, jive, blues, flamenco and even tap dancing), Ronnie Scott's is one of the city's most fashionable hang outs for cool hipsters, and a Mecca for fans of jazz, blues and soul.

Ronnie Scott's, 47 Frith St, W1D 4HT (020-7439 0747; www.ronniescotts.co.uk; Tottenham Court Rd tube; Mon-Sat 6pm-late, Sun noon-4pm, 6.30pm-midnight).

Wynton Marsalis

Roundhouse

Art meets architecture at the Roundhouse, one of London's legendary gig venues. Now Grade II* listed, it was constructed in 1847 as a Victorian steam-engine repair shed – round because it contained a railway turntable – and only became an arts venue in the '60s.

The Roundhouse was a showcase for many top bands in the '60s and '70s, from rock legends the Rolling Stones, Jimi Hendrix and Pink Floyd to punk stars like Patti Smith, the Clash and the Ramones, and witnessed some seminal musical moments – the Doors played their only UK gig here in 1968. It also hosted some of the more controversial theatrical performances of its day, including works by Peter Brook and the Living Theatre from New York. Kenneth Tynan's nude revue *Oh! Calcutta!* was launched here in 1970.

The venue closed in the early '80s and fell into disuse until it was bought in 1996 by Sir Torquil Norman who set up the Roundhouse Trust and undertook a £27 million redevelopment, completed in 2006. Since then the Roundhouse has been home to an exciting programme of cabaret, comedy, alternative theatre, dance, circus, installations and new media, and is once more one of the gems of the London gig circuit. It's large enough to attract quality

Coldplay

acts (capacity 3,300) but small enough for a great view of the stage (provided you avoid the pillars).

Roundhouse, Chalk Farm Rd, NW1 8EH (0300-6789 222; www.roundhouse.org.uk; Chalk Farm tube).

Royal Albert Hall

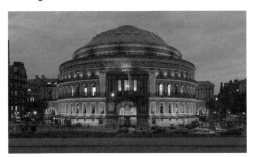

Opened by Queen Victoria in 1871, the Royal Albert Hall (Grade I listed) is one of the capital's most treasured historic buildings: an ornate Italianate concert hall with a distinctive glass and wrought-iron dome rising 135ft and facing Kensington Gardens. It was commissioned 'for the advancement of the Arts & Sciences and works of industry of all nations in fulfilment of the intention of Albert Prince Consort' – though sadly, Albert died ten years before its completion.

The Hall seats 5,272 and hosts some 400 shows a year, including classical music, rock and pop concerts, ballet, opera, film screenings with live orchestra, sports, awards ceremonies, school and community events, charity performances and banquets. It's probably best known as the stage for the celebrated BBC Proms concerts held annually each summer. The Proms were

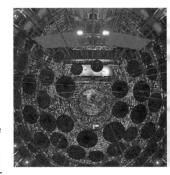

inaugurated in 1895 and are the world's longest running music festival, with daily classical music performances over eight weeks. They include more than 70 concerts in the Royal Albert Hall, plus chamber concerts at Cadogan Hall (see page 155). There are additional Proms in the Park events across the UK on the famous Last Night of the Proms.

You can take tours of the Royal Albert Hall, including its history, architecture and exclusive access to the Royal Retiring Room (see website for details and prices).

Royal Albert Hall, Kensington Gore, SW7 2AP (020-7589 8212; www.royalalberthall.com; Knightsbridge or S Kensington tube).

Shepherd's Bush Empire

Designed by pioneering theatre architect Frank Matcham and built in 1903 as a music hall, the Shepherd's Bush Empire (officially now the O2 Shepherd's Bush Empire) became the BBC Television Theatre in 1953 (home to *Hancock's Half Hour* and the *Old Grey Whistle Test* among other shows), but has operated as a music venue since 1991.

Brandon Flowers

With a capacity of 2,000 and decent sound pretty much everywhere, it's popular for 'small' and 'surprise' warm-up gigs. The Empire has witnessed performances from the likes of the Rolling Stones, Johnny Cash, Bob Dylan, Elvis Costello, the Sex Pistols, the Who, David Bowie, Blur, Bjork, Jeff Buckley, Bon Jovi, Take That, Adele, Amy Winehouse, the Cure, Kylie Minogue, Elton John, Oasis and Prince.

Shepherd's Bush Empire, Shepherd's Bush Grn, W12 8TT (020-8354 3300; www.academymusicgroup.com/ o2shepherdsbushempire; Shepherd's Bush Central/Market tube).

Troxy

Opened in 1933 as a grand Art Deco cinema – with a large sweeping staircase, chandeliers, floor to ceiling mirrors, thick carpets and a floodlit organ – the glamorous Troxy (Grade II listed) brought a touch of Hollywood to the East End. The cinema closed in 1960 and was used as a rehearsal space for the Royal Opera House in the '60s and '70s before becoming a bingo hall in the '80s.

Now restored to its former glory – including the installation of the mighty Wurlitzer theatre pipe organ that once graced the Trocadero Cinema in the Elephant and Castle – the 2,600-capacity Troxy is one of London's most versatile venues, hosting everything from live music to company conferences, sports events to weddings.

Troxy, 490 Commercial Rd, E1 0HX (020-7790 9000; www.troxy.co.uk; Limehouse DLR).

Union Chapel

Jeff Beck

Built in 1877, the Union Chapel is a vibrant community hub and award-winning venue that's a combination of working church, performance space and homeless shelter (with a bar and café). This architectural treasure (Grade II listed) is noted for its breath-taking Gothic interior, fantastic acoustics and superb organ (made by Henry Willis). The Chapel has been staging concerts and events since 1991 and since 2006 has hosted the annual Little Noise Sessions, featuring stripped-back sets by the likes of Amy Winehouse, Coldplay, and Florence and the Machine.

Union Chapel is also celebrated for its Margins Project for those who are homeless, isolated or in crisis, providing a range of services from workshops and advice to a café and shelter.

Union Chapel, 19b Compton Ter, N1 2UN (020-7226 1686; www.unionchapel.org.uk; Highbury & Islington rail).

Wigmore Hall

Built in 1901 by the German piano maker Bechstein next door to its showrooms, Wigmore Hall is one of the world's great concert halls, specialising in chamber and instrumental music, early music and song. Although small (seating 550), it's noted for its near perfect acoustics and striking Arts and Crafts interior, and was a favourite with many great 20th-century artists, in particular Benjamin Britten who premiered many of compositions here.

The Hall presents over 400 events a year, and in addition to being a platform for the world's most celebrated soloists and chamber musicians it also fosters the careers of talented young artists, with many making their first professional appearance in London on the Wigmore Hall's stage.

Wigmore Hall, 36 Wigmore St, W1U 2BP (020-7935 2141; http://wigmore-hall.org.uk; Bond St tube).

11.
Nightlife

As befits a 24-hour city, London has one of the world's most vibrant nightlife scenes. You can while away the hours of darkness with all manner of entertainment, from comedy, cabaret and burlesque to house, techno and electro, while sipping cocktails, watching celebrities and trying to slip into the VIP zone.

Occupying former theatres, railway arches, factories and warehouses, many of London's best-loved nightclubs started life as illegal party venues, and weekend all-night raves remain the lifeblood of many clubs. Some have a guest-list policy and strict dress code, while others have minimal attitude and allow you on the dance floor in your jeans. Theme nights are popular – check the music before you visit – and gigs by world-class DJs, many of whom found fame spinning the decks in London, are a huge draw.

If you're an inveterate clubber you'll know that nothing stays static in Clubland. London's ever-evolving nightlife will keep you royally entertained, from superclubs such as Heaven and the Ministry of Sound to more intimate venues and DJ bars. Whether you want to party with the A-list, have your ribs tickled by comedy's finest or party till breakfast time, you'll never be short of ideas in London.

Note that there's a crossover between live music venues (see **Chapter 10**) and nightclubs, and many clubs also feature live music gigs.

99 Club

One of London's best 'alternative' comedy clubs – and winner of the Chortle Award for Best Comedy Venue in London from 2011 to 2016 – the 99 Club is located at Ruby Blue nightclub in Leicester Square (next to the Odeon cinema). The club opened in 2004 above a pub on Great Windmill Street in a tiny room holding just 30 people, but within a few years it was

filling venues across the city. Today it stages shows every night of the week; club nights are Tuesday to Saturday at its flagship venue in Leicester Square, with other nights at companion venues in Covent Garden, Piccadilly Circus and Chinatown.

The critically acclaimed 99 Club has played host to nearly every major TV stand-up comedy act of recent years. It has a stellar reputation among both fans and comedians including Russell Howard, Lee Mack, Stephen K. Amos, Andy Parsons, Jason Manford, Rich Hall, Lenny Henry, John Bishop, Kevin Bridges, Jack Dee, Alan Carr, Lee Nelson, Patrick Monahan, Bob Mills and many more.

The standard ticket price includes entry to Ruby Blue (www.rubybluebar.co.uk) which opens at 5pm for pre-show meals and remains open till 3am (11pm Sundays).

99 Club, Ruby Blue, 28A Leicester Sq, WC2H 7LE (07760-488119; www.99clubcomedy.com; Leicester Sq tube; see website for programme and times).

Annabel's

The benchmark by which all London nightclubs are measured, Annabel's is an elegant private members' club and restaurant founded in 1963 by Mark Birley, who named it after his wife. Occupying a prime slot on Berkeley Square in Mayfair, the club's stellar reputation is founded on superb service and ambience, first-class cuisine and quality entertainment. The sumptuous interior – designed by Birley and Nina Campbell and recently updated by Birley's daughter, India Jane – includes a classy cocktail bar, dining room with a Moorish ceiling (there are also private dining rooms), unique starlit dance floor, courtyard garden and an outstanding collection of artwork.

Annabel's caters to an exclusive clientele. Frank Sinatra was allegedly one of the first celebrities to join and its illustrious list of (present and former) members includes representatives of the British Royal Family (including Princes Charles, William and Harry), heads of state such as Richard Nixon, plus legends of the film and music industries, from Jack Nicholson and Elizabeth Taylor to Mick Jagger and Shirley Bassey.

Members receive reciprocal membership of many of the world's leading nightclubs, a concierge service and access to special events, including live music performances, exclusive parties, dining experiences and cultural talks.

Annabel's, 44 Berkeley Sq, W1J 5QB (020-7629 1096; http://annabels.co.uk; Green Pk tube; Mon-Sat 8am-3pm, closed Sun).

Bethnal Green Working Men's Club

Another East End stalwart, the Bethnal Green Working Men's Club (opened in 1953) is the real deal: an old-fashioned working men's club that hasn't changed much since the '70s. Fortunately the entertainment has evolved, with regular social events, some racy, others more cultured, but most of all it's great fun! From dance classes, DJs and disco to karaoke, cabaret and bingo, the club is the natural home of local performance artists and one of the most creative and accessible venues in town, where audience participation is *de rigueur*.

There's also a basement bar serving inexpensive cocktails and beer brewed on site, alongside tasty food with a Franco-Spanish twist.

Bethnal Green Working Men's Club, 42-44 Pollard Row, E2 6NB (020-7739 7170; www.workersplaytime.net; Bethnal Grn tube; see website for programme & times).

Bonbonniere

Opened in 2014 in the heart of Mayfair, Bonbonniere (French for a small candy jar) was inspired by the lavish Fabergé egg commissioned by Russian nobleman Alexander Kelch in 1903, symbolising European opulence, status and wealth. Already one of the city's premier private members' nightclubs, it was acclaimed 'Best New Nightclub' at the 2015 London Club and Bar Awards. With sumptuous interiors, top international DJs, and a constant stream of celebrities and A-listers, Bonbonniere is renowned for entertaining the city's most fashionable clubbers.

A decadent box of delights, there's even a whimsical in-house sweet shop serving delectable candies and treats late into the wee hours.

Bonbonniere, 23 Orchard St, W1H 6HL (020-7935 4012; www.bonbonniereclub.com; Bond St tube; Tue and Fri-Sat 11pm-3am).

The Book Club

Located over two floors of a former Victorian warehouse, the Book Club interior blends the raw, pared-down character of a factory building with layers of bespoke furniture, mosaics and graphic lighting features, as well as constantly evolving art exhibitions adorning the walls. The many-faceted venue is a relaxing café by day and a buzzing club by night offering an eclectic programme of events and social activities including dance, art, music, film, talks, lectures, video-game nights and ping-pong tournaments.

However, it earns its place here courtesy of its hip basement bar and raunchy club nights featuring DJs such as Scroobius Pip, Roots Manuva, DJ EZ, Craig Charles and Norman Jay.

The Book Club, 100-106 Leonard St, EC2A 4RH (020-3889 8721; www.wearetbc.com; Shoreditch High St rail; Mon-Wed 8am-midnight, Thu-Fri 8am-2am, Sat 10am-2am, Sun 10am-midnight).

Café de Paris

First opened in Piccadilly in 1924, the Café de Paris is one of the most famous nightspots in the world and one of the best cabaret venues in London. It attracts the very best circus, burlesque, music, magic, cabaret and jazz acts, and is one of those places that everyone should visit at least once, if only to enjoy the extraordinary opulent baroque décor. Everyone from Madonna and the Spice Girls to *GQ* magazine and MTV has held a grand party here.

Recently restored, the spacious (capacity 700) venue has three separate bars in addition to the mezzanine and main dance floor.

Café de Paris, 3-4 Coventry St, W1D 6BL (020-7734 7700; www.cafedeparis.com; Piccadilly Circus tube; Fri-Sat 6pm-3am).

Cargo

A purpose-built venue in Shoreditch, atmospheric Cargo is nestled under disused railway arches and encompasses a nightclub, bar, restaurant and large outdoor courtyard. Since opening in 2000 it has presented a wide variety of music, ranging from live performances – from art punk and dubstep to psychedelic prog and wonk-pop – to full-on club nights with hot sounds including house, hip-hop, techno and electro.

The programme includes up-and-coming underground acts, big-name artists promoting new record releases and label parties, with gigs usually held seven days a week. The courtyard acts as a third room, where you can catch your breath away from the often crammed performance space and lounge/bar areas.

Cargo, 83 Rivington St, EC2A 3AY (020-7739 3440; www.cargo-london.com; Old St tube/ Shoreditch High St rail; see website for programme & times).

Cirque Le Soir

First opened in London in 2009, award-winning Cirque Le Soir has evolved into one of the most successful clubs in the world, offering a unique immersive experience. The circus-themed nightclub treats guests to a thrilling assault on the senses from every angle: dwarves, magicians, clowns, aerial acts, sword-swallowers, fire-eaters, burlesque dancers, snake charmers, acrobats, jugglers, contortionists and stilt walkers all feature among a host of weird and wonderful entertainment.

A place where the gorgeous and glamorous come to play, Cirque Le Soir has an electrifying and enchanting atmosphere, and is noted for its top DJs, expert mixologists and dazzling circus décor. There are sister clubs in Dubai and Shanghai.

Cirque Le Soir, 15-21 Ganton St, W1F 9BN (020-7287 8001; www.cirquelesoir.com; Oxford Circus tube; Mon, Wed, Fri-Sat 11pm-3am).

The Comedy Store

The daddy of all UK comedy clubs, the Comedy Store was opened in 1979 by Don Ward, who was inspired by similar venues he'd seen in the US. His fledgling club, then tucked above a strip joint in Soho, has grown into the most famous and respected brand in live comedy not just in London but worldwide, attracting some 3,500 punters a week.

During the '80s, the Comedy Store was *the* home of 'alternative comedy'. Radical young comedians (now household names) such as Alexei Sayle, Rik Mayall, Adrian Edmonson, Jennifer Saunders, Dawn French, Keith Allen, Peter Richardson, Nigel Planer and Arnold Brown cut their teeth on the Comedy Store's stage, with the likes of Clive Anderson and Ben Elton hot on their heels.

The Store's regular show programme includes everything from topical news-based comedy from the Cutting Edge team (Tuesdays) to the very best in Comedy 'Improv' from the Comedy Store Players (Wednesdays and Sundays), including Paul Merton and Josie Lawrence. From Thursdays to Saturdays, the stage is reserved for the Best in Stand Up: classic stand-up comedy featuring some of the finest talent from around the globe, with late shows on Fri-Sat. The last Monday of every month is a real crowd pleaser: the Gong Show gives would-be stand ups an open mic for as long as the audience will allow.

The Comedy Store, 1A Oxendon St, SW1Y 4EE (0844-871 7699; http://thecomedystore.co.uk/london; Piccadilly Circus tube; Mon-Thu 6.30-11pm, Fri-Sat 6pm-2am, Sun 6-11pm).

Drama

Formerly known as Whisky Mist, Drama – the brainchild of entrepreneurs Nick House of Mahiki and Ryan Bish/Tom Berg of Cirque Le Soir – is located at the prestigious Hilton Hotel on Park Lane. Opened in 2015, it's one of the city's newest and most exciting nightspots, with its striking artwork and dramatic décor, and a state-of-the-art Funktion One sound system.

This theatrical club features a gold room, a wall made from Japanese beckoning cat figurines (*Maneki-Neko*) and banana-scented scratch-and-sniff wallpaper in the Ladies' loos, while champagne is served from neon supermarket trolleys. It numbers Leonardo DiCaprio, Naomi Campbell and Usain Bolt among its clientele.

Drama, 35 Hertford St, W1J 7SD (020-7208 4125; www.dramaparklane.com; Green Pk/Hyde Pk Corner tube; Thu-Sun 11pm-3am).

DSTRKT

Opened in 2011 at a reputed cost of £25 million, DSTRKT is an exclusive restaurant and club a stone's throw from Piccadilly Circus. A serial winner at the London Club & Bar Awards, this glamorous club features a decadent lounge (with a bar made of precious black stone), state-of-the-art sound and lighting systems, and a stage where the likes of Snoop Dog, Drake, Afrojack, The Weeknd, Wiz Khalifa, Inna, LMFAO, Sean Paul and P Diddy have performed.

A 'bit' expensive for a girls' night out – a huge Methuselah bottle of champagne will set you back around £30,000 – but a great place for a few cocktails and some tasty food.

DSTRKT, 9 Rupert St, W1D 6DG (020-7317 9120; www.dstrkt.co.uk; Piccadilly Circus tube; Mon-Sat, restaurant/bar 5pm-2am, Tue-Sat lounge 11pm-3am, closed Sun).

Egg London

A vast warehouse-style venue north of King's Cross spread over three floors with five areas, including an enormous main dance floor, huge open-air terrace and a garden – and a 24-hour licence for all-night parties (breakfast and coffee is served, too!) – Egg is a nightspot like no other. Despite its vast size, the club has quite an intimate atmosphere, with superb sound and lighting, and some of the capital's best music and DJs.

The list of international and home-grown superstars that have mixed sounds here here reads like a who's who of DJ talent: Laurent Garnier, Solomun, Derrick May, David Morales, Dubfire, Matthias Tanzmann, Guti, Danny Tengalia, Dennis Ferrer, Nicole Moudaber, Kevin Saunderson, Matador, Lee Foss, Lefoeh, Amine Edge & Dance, Juan Atkins and Kerri Chandler, to name but a few.

There are few clubs that present house music (in all its genres) as well as Egg, which also dips into techno and disco. The club offers an eclectic mix of nights – regular event nights including Paradox, Supernova, Circus, Fact and Egg Presents – and also hosts popular events with DJs and vocalists from the glory days of acid house, Balearic and rave.

Egg London, 200 York Way, N7 9AX (020-7871 7111; www.egglondon.co.uk; Caledonian Rd tube/rail; Tue 11pm-6am, Fri 11pm-7am, Sat 11pm-9am).

Electric Brixton

After a £1 million refit, former rave palace The Fridge reopened in 2011 as Electric Brixton, housed in a converted Art Deco cinema next to Lambeth Town Hall. With room for some 1,700 ravers, it's now a leading nightclub venue – with a high-tech sound system and classy interior design – hosting weekly club nights, top guest DJ sets (Felix Da Housecat, Kissy Sell Out, Beardyman, Gilles Peterson, Glitch Mob, etc.) and an eclectic programme of live gigs.

Set over two floors with a sweeping balcony, the Electric is compact but packs a mega punch, a bit like a mini Brixton Academy (see page 154) but with a personality all its own.

Electric Brixton, Town Hall Parade, SW2 1RJ (020-7274 2290; http://electricbrixton.uk.com; Brixton tube; see website for programme & times).

Fire

Sprawled across ten railway arches in Vauxhall, Fire is a huge industrial-style nightclub with a series of neon-lit rooms, an outdoor terrace and bar, and an amazing (Funktion One) sound system. The club claims to be south London's leading nightclub and features world class DJs – including sets from Ms Dynamite, John Digweed, Trevor Jackson, Skream, Booka Shade, AME, Apollonia and Jackmaster – spinning the best in cutting-edge house, techno, bass, dubstep and more.

Thanks to their super-late licence, Fire is open until the crack of dawn, which means no waiting around for early morning trains to take you home after a night of hard clubbing.

Fire, 39 Parry St, SW8 1RT (020-3242 0040; www. firelondon.net; Vauxhall tube; see website for events & times).

The Grand

Occupying a huge iconic Victorian theatre in Clapham, originally a music hall (1900), the 1,250-capacity Grand (also called the Clapham Grand/London Grand) is one of southwest London's best clubs. It hosts an eclectic programme of events, ranging from club nights and live gigs to comedy, theatre and bingo, set in one of the capital's most beautiful and historic venues.

Weekends at the Grand are all about partying, when top London promoters host events such as Rebel Bingo, Ultimate Anthems and Shorebitch, while on club nights (selected Fridays and Saturdays) resident DJs play a great mix of party classics from hip-hop to house, disco to R&B and everything in between.

The Grand, 21-25 St John's Hill, SW11 1TT (020-7223 6523; www.claphamgrand.com; Clapham Jct rail; see website for programme & times).

Heaven

London's first gay superclub, Heaven opened in 1979 in the arches beneath Charing Cross station, the brainchild of club entrepreneur Jeremy Norman. It was revolutionary in its day, the birthplace of Hi-NRG and acid house, and a magnet for gay celebrities, putting on the most spectacular stage shows in town. Heaven quickly became the focal point for what had (until then) been a fairly understated gay scene.

The music policy at Heaven – now also a gig venue and popular with straights as well as gays – changed from trance and house to bubbly commercial pop in 2008, when it went into partnership with G-A-Y, but it has maintained its popularity and is packed out most nights of the week.

Heaven, Under the Arches, Villiers St, WC2N 6NG (0844-847 2351; www.heaven-live.co.uk; Embankment tube; see website for programme & times).

Koko

Opened in 2005, Koko is the latest in a long line of musical venues to occupy this Camden hotspot. The original building opened in 1900 as a music hall and did stints as a theatre, cinema and rock venue – during the '70s it was the Music Machine, a punk and heavy metal stronghold – until in 1982 it morphed into the Camden Palace, home of the New Romantics and the venue (in 1983) for Madonna's first London show.

It was extensively refurbished in 2004, reinstating much of the building's original palatial decor (deep-red walls topped with a huge glitter ball) while also creating a first-class 21st-century entertainment venue. Without a doubt, Koko – as it's been since 2005 – is one of London's most eye-catching clubs.

It's a live music venue as well as a club, and many legends have graced Koko's stage: Coldplay held their celeb-filled *X&Y* album launch here, while Prince and Ed Sheeran have played secret shows. Other stars to perform at Koko include Roxy Music, the Red Hot Chilli Peppers, Paul Weller, Oasis, Amy Winehouse, Lady Gaga, Kanye West and many more.

Regular club nights include Club NME on Fridays and Guilty Pleasures on the last Saturday of the month.

Koko, 1A Camden High St, NW1 7JE (020-7388 3222; www.koko.uk.com; Mornington Cres. tube; see website for programme & times).

The Ministry of Sound

Opened by Justin Berkmann in 1991 in a former bus depot as an alcohol-free venue dedicated to house music, the legendary Ministry of Sound in Elephant & Castle was one of the world's first super clubs and arguably the most famous. It has grown into a multimedia entertainment brand, including various record labels, television, radio, a clothing company and sister clubs across the globe.

Boasting a massive sound system, three dance floors (The Box, 103 and Baby Box), three bars, VIP lounges and a star line-up of big name DJs, the club attracts thousands of clubbers south of the Thames every weekend. A wide range of external and in-house promotions have dictated the music policy down the years, with everything from house and garage through to trance, techno and electro house.

Once the epitome of warehouse cool, the Ministry's best days are behind it, although it still holds its own with most clubs and

the music is still thumpingly good – every self-respecting dance fan should visit at least once. It was recently refurbished and revamped with an uprated sound system and an injection of much needed DJ creativity.

Ministry of Sound, 103 Gaunt St, SE1 6DP (020-7740 8600; www.ministryofsound.com; Elephant & Castle tube; see website for events & times).

Montezuma

Launched in 2015 and named after the last Aztec emperor, Montezuma is a beautiful lounge and nightclub in South Kensington, winner of the London Club & Bar Awards 'Best Boutique Club London 2016'. With its magnificent golden Aztec décor, an eclectic cocktail list, state-of-the-art sound and lighting systems, and some of the capital's best DJs spinning house, deep house and techno (along with hip-hop and R&B), it adds up to one cool club atmosphere and a welcome addition to the local club scene.

Montezuma is sexy, young and fresh, which along with its late night licence and stunning intimate setting, make it a must visit for high-flying party animals.

Montezuma, 17A Harrington Rd, SW7 3ES (020-7589 0990; http://montezumalondon.com; S Kensington tube; Thu-Sat 10pm-3am).

Proud Camden

Located in the former 19th-century equine hospital in Camden's Stables Market, Proud Camden is a relaxing gallery space and bar by day (www.proudonline.co.uk) and a lively burlesque and cabaret venue after dark. This lovely Grade II listed building was a stronghold for live bands and the alternative scene for many years, but has been transformed into a glamorous nightclub with cutting-edge music nights, live performances and a cabaret supper club. The original stables are now private (bookable) VIP spaces, each named after a famous racehorse, from Red Rum to Sea Biscuit

Elegant, original and fun, Proud Camden is a special destination for a night out.

Proud Camden, The Horse Hospital, Stables Market, Chalk Farm Rd, NW1 8AH (020-7482 3867; http://proudcamden.com; Camden Town tube; see website for programme & times).

Rah Rah Room

Previously home to the Electric Carousel (and, further back, the legendary Pigalle Supper Club), this kitsch corner of St James's is now the base for the raucous Rah Rah Room (nightclub, bar and restaurant) with its magnificent murals, fabulous light-art projections and plethora

of red velvet. On Fridays and Saturdays roll up for the Kitsch Cabaret, a blend of old-school music hall and Las Vegas floorshow, classic revue entertainment with a modern twist: live singing, quick-fire repartee, high-kicking glamour and belting show stoppers.

When the curtains close you can let your hair down and party late into the night as cabaret becomes club, with top DJs ensuring hot sounds. The Rah Rah Room also hosts live music events – see website for information.

Rah Rah Room, 215-217 Piccadilly, W1J 9HN (020-3588 1111; www.rahrahroom.com; Piccadilly Circus tube; Thu, Sun 10pm-4am, Fri-Sat 6pm-4am).

Royal Vauxhall Tavern

A former Victorian music hall (Grade II listed and dating from 1863) situated in Vauxhall (where else?), the notorious Royal Vauxhall Tavern has been a gay venue since the Second World War, hosting club nights and drag acts. It's the spiritual heart of Vauxhall's gay village where a busy midweek programme sees it packed every night for bingo, comedy and music, while at weekends queues stretch round the block for the world-class drag acts, burlesque and generally risqué shows.

Straights are welcome at the Royal Vauxhall tavern, but those of a more delicate disposition should be aware that there's a *lot* of audience participation!

Royal Vauxhall Tavern, 372 Kennington Ln, SE11 5HY (020-7820 1222; www.vauxhalltavern. com; Vauxhall tube/rail; see website for opening times).

Scala

A nightclub, music and arts venue close to King's Cross/St Pancras stations, plush Scala is the most recent reincarnation of the old King's Cross Cinema, which opened in 1920. It switched from family entertainment to adult films in the '70s, before becoming a live music venue where Iggy Pop and Hawkwind strutted their stuff and, later, an art-house cinema.

Here since 1999, Scala is one of London's most spacious venues – with room for 1,150 revellers, spread over four floors, with three bars, two dance floors and a stage – offering a wide range of music, e.g. indie, electro, hip-hop, R&B and folk. It's a great place to see up-and-coming bands as well as established stars.

Scala, 275 Pentonville Rd, N1 9NL (020-7833 2022; http://scala.co.uk; King's Cross/St Pancras tube/rail; see website for events & times).

Windmill International

Starting life as the Britain's first art-house cinema in 1909, the Palais de Luxe changed direction in 1932, becoming the infamous Windmill Theatre. This revue theatre was best known for its nude *tableaux vivants* – naked girls in stationary postures – obeying the licensing laws that dictated 'If it moves it's rude'. The Windmill stayed open throughout the Second World War but closed in 1964, becoming a cinema and later a nightclub.

It was reincarnated as the Windmill International in the mid '90s and is now one of London's most exciting gentlemen's clubs, employing over 60 dancers (the 'Windmill Girls') from around the world, who perform in lingerie or fully nude to different themes.

Windmill International, 17-19 Great Windmill St, W1D 7JZ (020-7439 3558; www. windmillinternational.com; Piccadilly Circus tube; Mon-Sat 9pm-5.30am, closed Sun).

XOYO

One of East London's top live music clubs, XOYO in Shoreditch opened in 2010 and is a Victorian loft-style building with oodles of space (it holds 800 people), an underground vibe and a growing reputation among ravers: it was voted one of the world's Top 100 Clubs by *DJ Magazine* in 2014 and 2015. The club's split-level design includes a basement

with a stage and a more intimate upstairs bar. Hosting live bands throughout the week and top DJs (along with up-and-coming turntable artists) spinning house, techno and disco, it's one of the capital's top dance experiences, offering cutting-edge sound and light.

On Friday nights the club stages a programme of live events, while Saturdays are dedicated to parties from some of London's top club promoters. An aspirational platform, uber-cool XOYO runs a regular residency series, engaging top DJs for three month seasons to host the club's Saturday night programme, alongside special guests. Famous DJ acts have ranged from Eats Everything, Jackmaster

and Tiga to Simian Mobile Disco, Heidi and Andy C.

Outside of the club's packed weekend diary, XOYO also plays host to an eclectic and forward-thinking selection of live gigs and student nights.

XOYO, 32-37 Cowper St, EC2A 4AP (020-7608 2878; www.xoyo.co.uk; Old St tube/rail; see website for events & times).

12.
Parks & Gardens

It may be a metropolis and home to more than 8.5 million people, but no other city in Britain has such a rich diversity of beautiful green spaces as London. The capital's green bounty includes magnificent royal parks, historic garden cemeteries, breath-taking country parks, expansive commons, tropical greenhouse collections, elegant squares and enchanting 'secret' gardens, many known only to insiders and locals.

London is more verdant than any other world city of its size – green spaces cover almost 40 per cent of Greater London – and provides a wealth of places where you can play, relax, exercise and commune with nature year round. There are around 400 green spaces in the City of London alone and over 1,000 in Greater London, ranging from famous public parks to semi-private gardens, city farms to converted churchyards – each with its own unique character. This chapter features 20 of the city's best parks and gardens, including major attractions such as Hyde and Regent's Parks, and some that are less well known – but just as glorious – like delightful St Dunstan-in-the-East and Hill Garden. And most can be enjoyed completely free of charge.

So, whether you're a nature lover or a history buff, a horticulturist or a fitness freak, or just a deckchair dreamer looking for a bit of peace and quiet, you'll find your perfect spot in one of London's parks.

Battersea Park

Opened in 1858, Battersea Park is a delightful 200-acre public park situated on the south bank of the River Thames opposite Chelsea. With the completion of the new Chelsea Bridge (opened in 1858) the park became a major attraction and was a unique destination until well into the 20th century. Today, it's home to a small aviary, boating lake, bandstand and several all-weather sports facilities – including tennis courts, a running track and soccer pitches – a children's zoo and the Pump House Gallery, plus two cafés.

Rarely has an inner-city park contained so many hidden secrets, variety and simple enjoyment, and it's considered by many to be the city's most interesting major park.

Battersea Park, Albert Bridge Rd, SW11 4NJ (020-8871 7530/020-8871 6000; www. wandsworth.gov.uk/batterseapark and http:// batterseapark.org; Battersea Park rail; daily 8am-dusk; free).

Brompton Cemetery

One of London's 'Magnificent Seven' (see **Highgate Cemetery** on page 191) cemeteries, Brompton (39 acres) is one of Britain's oldest and most distinguished garden cemeteries (Grade I listed), containing some 35,000 monuments (many listed) adorning over 200,000 burial sites. Brompton is the only Crown Cemetery still used for burials, although it's more popular as a public park than a place to mourn the dead. Noted for its beautiful trees, particularly lime trees along the northwest and southeast avenues, with scattered mature weeping silver lime, holly, holm oak, cedar of Lebanon and yew.

As well as its many attractions, the cemetery provides an oasis in all seasons and is a haven of peace and tranquillity.

Brompton Cemetery, Fulham Rd, SW10 9UG (020-7352 1201; www.royalparks.org.uk/parks/ brompton-cemetery and www.brompton-cemetery.org; W Brompton tube; see website for opening times; free).

Cannizaro Park

One of London's loveliest green 'secrets', Cannizaro is a Grade II* listed park of 35 acres on the edge of Wimbledon Common. A private garden for some 300 years, opened to the public in 1949, it combines great natural beauty with a unique collection of rare and exquisite trees and shrubs, including sassafras, camellia, rhododendron and other ericaceous plants.

The park has a large variety of green areas from expansive lawns to small intimate spaces such as the herb and tennis court gardens, and lovely leisurely walks through woodlands. Formal areas have been developed, with a sunken garden next to Cannizaro House Hotel and an Italian garden near the pond.

Cannizaro Park, West Side Common, Wimbledon, SW19 4UE (020-8545 3678; www. cannizaropark.com; Wimbledon tube/rail; daily 8am-dusk; free).

Green Park

The smallest of the royal parks, open to the public since 1826, Green Park may appear to be an extension of St James's Park (see page 199), but the two have very different characters. If St James's Park is an urban garden, Green Park is lush pasture: peaceful, relaxing and very green. Encompassing just 47 acres, it's an important link in a chain of parks stretching from Kensington to Westminster – the green lungs of central London.

Today, it's a popular venue for picnics, sunbathing, walking and jogging. There are no formal sports or playgrounds and no lake for wildlife, although there are common birds such as blackbirds, starlings and tits and, in winter, migrant birds such as redwing and fieldfare.

Green Park, SW1A 2BJ (0300-061 2350; www. royalparks.org.uk/parks/green-park; Green Pk tube; unrestricted access; free).

Greenwich Park

Greenwich Park (Grade I listed) is London's most interesting and varied royal park, rich in historic buildings, museums, galleries, monuments, gardens and wildlife. It extends to 183 acres – one of the largest green spaces in southeast London – and has been open to the general public since 1830. Greenwich is

also London's oldest royal park and has some of the capital's most impressive views across the Thames towards Docklands and the City.

The park is part of the Greenwich World Heritage Site – which provides a setting for several historic buildings, including the Old Royal Observatory, the Royal Naval College, the National Maritime Museum and the Queen's House – and offers a wealth of amenities and facilities for entertainment, recreation and sport.

Greenwich Park, Greenwich, SE10 8QY (0300-061 2380; www.royalparks.org. uk/parks/greenwich-park and www. friendsofgreenwichpark.org.uk; Cutty Sark DLR; 6am-dusk; free).

Hampstead Heath

Hampstead Heath is a large, ancient park between Hampstead and Highgate, extending to 790 acres and sitting astride one of the city's highest points (440ft). Rambling and hilly, it's one of London's most beloved open spaces, encompassing grassland, woodlands, gardens, ponds, playgrounds and a profusion of sports facilities, attracting over 7 million visitors a year.

The Heath is home to a range of activities and sports and is extensively used by walkers, runners, swimmers, horse-riders and kite flyers. Swimming takes place all year round in two of its three natural swimming ponds: the men's pond, which opened in the 1890s, and the ladies' pond that opened in 1925.

Hampstead Heath, Spaniards Rd, NW3 7JJ (020-7332 3322; www.cityoflondon.gov.uk > green spaces, www.hampsteadheath.net and www. hampsteadheath.org.uk; Hampstead/Golders Grn tube; unrestricted access; free).

Highgate Cemetery

Opened in 1839 soon after Queen Victoria's accession to the throne, Highgate Cemetery (Grade I listed) was one of London's 'Magnificent Seven' cemeteries, built in the 19th century to relieve overcrowded parish burial grounds. Highgate is probably the best known and most fashionable of these cemeteries, due to its stunning architecture and unparalleled elevation overlooking London.

The cemetery covers an area of 37 acres and is divided into two parts – the original West Cemetery and the East Cemetery, which opened in 1856. The former is accessible only by guided tour to protect the monuments and for the public's safety, while the latter can be visited independently and remains open for burials.

Highgate Cemetery, Swain's Ln, N6 6PJ (020-8340 1834; http://highgatecemetery.org; Highgate/Archway tube; see website for opening hours & fees).

Hill Garden & Pergola

Charming Hill Garden and its beautiful pergola (Grade II listed) are among the hidden delights of Hampstead Heath. This formal Arts and Crafts garden was created between 1906 and 1925 by celebrated landscape architect Thomas Mawson for the soap magnate Lord Leverhulme (1851-1925).

In late spring and early summer the raised, covered pergola – 800ft in length – is festooned with fragrant flowers including jasmine, buddleia, sage, honeysuckle, vines, clematis, kiwi, potato vine, lavender and wisteria. Visit during the early evening and you may even see roosting long-eared bats. In contrast to the wild decadence of the pergola, Hill Garden is beautifully manicured and a slice of paradise, offering panoramic views over London.

Hill Garden & Pergola, Inverforth Cl, off North End Way, NW3 7EX (www.cityoflondon.gov.uk > green spaces > Hampstead Heath > heritage; Golders Grn or Hampstead tube; daily 8.30am-dusk; free).

Holland Park & Kyoto Garden

London's most romantic park, Holland Park (54 acres) was formerly the grounds of Cope Castle, a large Jacobean mansion dating from the early 17th century; later renamed Holland House, it was largely destroyed by bombing during the Second World War. It's one of the capital's smallest public parks, but has plenty to offer: beautiful views, gardens, sports areas, peacocks, an ecology centre, some of the city's best children's play facilities, a café, large areas of woodland and a Japanese garden. The park is also a much-loved picnic spot, with plenty of secluded hideaways in a variety of environments.

One of the highlights of Holland Park is the beautiful Kyoto Garden, a Japanese garden donated by the Chamber of Commerce in Kyoto in 1991 to celebrate the Japan Festival, which was held in London in 1992. Refurbished in 2001, the garden is immaculately kept and widely regarded as one of the capital's most tranquil corners. It has a lovely pond with stepping stones and a 15ft waterfall, and is surrounded by elegant plantings of Japanese shrubs and trees, offering an ever-changing variety of vivid colours.

In summer, opera performances are staged by Opera Holland Park (www.operahollandpark.com) under a temporary canopy, with the ruins of Holland House as a backdrop.

Holland Park & Kyoto Garden, Ilchester Pl, W8 6LU (www.rbkc.gov.uk/leisure-and-culture/parks/ holland-park; Kensington High St/Notting Hill tube; daily 7.30am-dusk; free).

Hyde Park

The largest of the four great royal parks that run like a ribbon of green through central London, Hyde Park is a major London landmark, attracting millions of visitors a year. In past times it has hosted exhibitions and celebrations, witnessed protests and executions, and provided respite from the noise and discomforts of the city – as, indeed, it still does. Covering an area of 350 acres, it borders Kensington Gardens (see page 194) to the west – although the two parks appear to be a seamless extension of each other, they have been separate entities since 1728.

Hyde Park has a wide variety of flora and fauna. Robins and tits nest among the trees and in herbaceous plantings such as the Rose Garden, while in the centre of the park a wilderness meadow attracts butterflies to its wildflowers, and waterfowl share the Serpentine with pleasure boats and swimmers. The park is full of unexpected treats – memorials, statues and works of art – including numerous well-loved attractions.

Many major events have taken place in Hyde Park. In 1851 it was the venue for the Great Exhibition – Joseph Paxton's Crystal Palace was first built here – and more recently has hosted concerts by artists from the Rolling Stones to Pavarotti, and it also provided a venue for sporting events at the 2012 Olympics.

Hyde Park, W2 2UH (0300-061 2114; www. royalparks.org.uk/parks/hyde-park; Lancaster Gate, Marble Arch, Hyde Park Corner or Knightsbridge tube; daily 5am-midnight; free).

Kensington Gardens

The quieter, more refined neighbour of Hyde Park, Kensington Gardens strikes just the right balance between culture and nature. It was once the 'back garden' of Kensington Palace, one of the city's great royal residences, although its 270 acres are now open to all. Divided from Hyde Park in the 18th century, Kensington Gardens has a more formal atmosphere – it's hard

to imagine a rock concert taking place here – and the gardens, fenced off and closed at sunset, feel more private. The main attraction in Kensington Gardens is Kensington Palace (www.hrp.org.uk/Kensington-palace). Re-launched in 2012 following a £12m facelift, it's a charming and well-presented stately home, featuring a magnificent sunken garden planted in 1908 to recreate the splendour of the original 17th-century gardens.

Kensington Gardens, W2 2UH (0300-061 2000; www.royalparks.org.uk/parks/kensington-gardens; Lancaster Gate/Queensway tube; daily 6am-sunset; free).

Morden Hall Park

Owned by the National Trust, Morden Hall Park encompasses over 125 acres of parkland in what was once rural Surrey. This tranquil former deer park is one of the few remaining estates that lined the River Wandle during its industrial heyday, and contains Morden Hall itself, a stable yard (now restored and containing interactive exhibitions), pretty Morden Cottage situated in the rose garden, and many old farm buildings, some of which house a garden centre and a city farm.

Visitors can still see the conserved (original) waterwheel that, until 1922, turned the massive millstones used to crush tobacco into fine powder (snuff).

Morden Hall Park, Morden Hall Rd, Morden, SM4 5JD (020-8545 6850; www.nationaltrust.org.uk/morden-hall-park; Morden tube; daily dawn-dusk; free).

Postman's Park

A short distance north of St Paul's Cathedral is one of the City of London's largest parks (although still tiny), best known as the site of a poignant memorial. Postman's Park – the name reflects its popularity with (and use by) workers from the nearby Post Office headquarters – stands on the old burial ground of St Botolph's Aldersgate, and is a peaceful refuge in the City.

In 1900 it became the site of the Memorial to Heroic Self Sacrifice, the brainchild of George Frederic Watts, where over 50 plaques tell the tales of selfless sacrifice; an inspiring and poignant tribute to 'ordinary' people.

Postman's Park, Saint Martin's Le-Grand, EC1A (020-7374 4127; www.cityoflondon.gov.uk > things to do > green spaces > city gardens > parks and gardens; St Paul's tube; daily 8am-dusk; free).

Queen Mary's Gardens

Tucked away in the Inner Circle of Regent's Park, Queen Mary's Gardens – named after the wife of King George V – were laid out in 1932. It's London's largest and best formal rose garden containing over 400 different varieties in separate and mixed beds, and a total of some 30,000 plants. It's a honey-pot for garden lovers (and bees) in spring and summer, when tens of thousands of plants are in bloom.

In summer, the gardens plays host to the Open Air Theatre (http://openairtheatre. com), a permanent venue with a three- to four-month summer season. The gardens also contain the Garden Café, serving teas, coffees and lunch, plus summer suppers.

Queen Mary's Gardens, Inner Circle, Regent's Pk, NW1 4NR (020-7486 7905/0300-061 2000; www.royalparks.org.uk/parks/the-regents-park/ things-to-see-and-do/gardens-and-landscapes/ queen-marys-gardens; Baker St tube; daily dawn-dusk; free).

Regent's Park

Home to London Zoo, a vast swathe of parkland and some of the most exquisite Georgian terraces in the city, Regent's Park is the largest of central London's five royal parks. It was created in the early 19th century for the Prince Regent

– later King George IV – and is officially titled *The* Regent's Park. These days, it's better known for its sporting and entertainment facilities and wealth of birdlife, although the glorious architecture that surrounds the park is a constant reminder of its noble heritage.

Regent's Park covers 410 acres and is encircled by Regent's Canal, built to link the Grand Union Canal to the London docks, which offers a peaceful towpath stroll to Camden Lock (east) or west to Little Venice. The park has an unusual layout consisting of two ring roads: the Outer and Inner Circles. The Inner Circle encloses formal gardens and an open-air theatre, while the Outer Circle surrounds the wilder reaches of the park and its many amenities, which

include gardens, a boating lake, sports pitches, playgrounds and, of course, the famous zoo.

Regent's Park contains some glorious formal gardens, including Queen Mary's Gardens (see page 195), the Avenue Gardens in the south eastern corner, and the Garden of St John's Lodge.

Regent's Park, NW1 4NR (0300-061 2300; www. royalparks.org.uk/parks/the-regents-park; Baker St, Regent's Pk or Great Portland St tube; daily 5am-sunset; free)

Richmond Park

Richmond Park is the most extensive royal park in London and the second-largest urban park in Europe, extending to 2,360 acres. It's classified as a European Special Area of Conservation, a National Nature Reserve and a Site of Special Scientific Interest – with a plethora of flora and fauna – and is famous for its deer, which number around 650.

The park is enclosed by a high brick wall – Grade II listed and 8 miles in length – with a dozen gates, allowing access to pedestrians and motor vehicles. Cars are only permitted during daylight hours, and no commercial vehicles apart from taxis are allowed entry. Pedestrians and cyclists have 24-hour access, except when there's a deer cull, and the park also has designated bridleways for horse riders and cycle paths.

Despite its proximity to London and some of the capital's busiest roads, Richmond Park can still feel like a wilderness – especially under the canopy of one of the many woods and spinneys, or on a misty morning when you glimpse a stag gazing back at you, antlers outlined against the sky.

The park has many highlights, including the Isabella Plantation, a stunning ornamental woodland garden extending to 42 acres south of Pen Ponds. It's managed organically resulting in rich flora and fauna, and is jam-packed with exotic plants and worth visiting all year round.

Richmond Park, Richmond, TW10 5HS (0300-061 2200; www.royalparks.org.uk/parks/richmond-park and www.frp.org.uk; Richmond tube/rail then bus; unrestricted access; free).

Royal Botanic Gardens, Kew

The Royal Botanic Gardens, Kew – better known simply as Kew Gardens – comprise around 300 acres of gardens and botanical greenhouses. Created in 1759, they're the world's most famous botanical gardens, welcoming over 2 million visitors annually, and have been a UNESCO World Heritage Site since 2003. Kew houses the world's largest and most diverse botanical collection, including reference collections, and contains some 50,000 plants from all over the world, including over 14,000 trees, while the Herbarium has over 7 million specimens.

Kew Gardens cannot be appreciated in one visit and reveals something new every time you visit, with areas devoted to all types of flora, from azaleas and bluebells to roses and rhododendrons.

Royal Botanic Gardens, Kew, TW9 3AB (020-8332 5655; www.kew.org; Kew Gdns tube; see website for opening times & fees).

St Dunstan-in-the-East Garden

The 12th-century church of St Dunstan-in-the-East was largely destroyed in the Blitz of 1941, although a tower and steeple added in the late 17th century by Sir Christopher Wren survived intact. The Corporation of London acquired the Grade I listed ruins, which were incorporated into a garden opened in 1971.

Today, St Dunstan's is one of the City's loveliest gardens and a welcome retreat from the surrounding bustle. Visitors can enjoy a huge variety of plants wending their way around the ruins; the walls and majestic windows have been draped and decorated with Virginia creeper and ornamental vine, which turn crimson in the autumn.

St Dunstan-in-the-East Garden, St Dunstan's Hill, EC3R 5DD (020-7332 3505; www. cityoflondon.gov.uk > things to do > green spaces > city gardens > parks and gardens; Monument tube; daily 8am-dusk; free).

St James's Park

The oldest of London's royal parks, St James's Park is surrounded by three great palaces: the Palace of Westminster (now the Houses of Parliament), St James's Palace and Buckingham Palace. The park is relatively small (57 acres) and has a tranquil lake at its centre with a small island at either end, surrounded by lawns and trees. It's a glorious urban landscape, providing relaxation and recreation for local residents, tourists and workers.

You can hire a deckchair by the bandstand (with free concerts on summer evenings), watch the resident pelicans being fed, or take the circular stroll around the lake, part of the Diana Memorial Walk which begins at Kensington Palace.

St James's Park, SW1A 2BJ (0300-061 2350; www.royalparks.org.uk/parks/st-jamess-park; St James's Pk tube; daily 5am-midnight; free).

York House Gardens

York House (Grade II listed) is a fine 17th-century building with a fascinating history, set in beautiful grounds on the banks of the River Thames. The gardens were commissioned by Sir Ratan Tata (1871-1918), who installed striking statues of naked female figures – representing the Oceanides or sea nymphs of Greek mythology – in highly unusual attitudes.

Around the recently restored cascades, planting has been designed to harmonise with the statues, with greens, pinks and whites predominating. Some unusual specimen trees and shrubs enliven the landscaping, including several types of magnolia, *cornus contraversa* (wedding cake tree) and tulip trees, and there's also a beautifully restored Japanese garden.

York House Gardens, Sion Rd, Twickenham, TW1 3DD (020-8891 1411; www.richmond.gov.uk > services > parks and open spaces and www. yorkhousesociety.org.uk; Twickenham rail; Mon-Sat 7.30am-dusk, Sun 9am-dusk; free).

13.
Places of Worship

London has a wealth of glorious ancient churches and cathedrals. Anglican and nonconformist churches and chapels predominate, but there are also many Catholic churches as well as places of worship for the great non-Christian religions, including Islam, Hinduism and Judaism.

London's largest concentration of historic churches is in the City of London, despite substantial losses during the Blitz: most date from the 17th and 18th centuries (many older churches were lost during the Great Fire of 1666) and are Grade I or Grade II* listed. Many (including St Paul's) are the work of England's finest architect, Sir Christopher Wren, and his various associates including Nicholas Hawksmoor and Robert Hooke.

Most people are familiar with the dominant landmarks of Westminster Abbey and St. Paul's Cathedral, although there are dozens of equally awe-inspiring churches in the capital, rich in history, architectural beauty, art, genealogy and spiritual significance – and most are free to visit. From the ebullient Brompton Oratory and elegant St Stephen Walbrook to the wedding-cake splendour of the Hindu Neasden Temple, each provides a peaceful place for worship and reflection, or simply somewhere to escape the hustle and bustle of the city. Along with regular services, many churches offer lunchtime/evening music recitals and excellent cafés.

All Hallows by the Tower

All Hallows by the Tower is an ancient Grade I listed church – built on the site of a Roman building, of which there are traces in the Crypt Museum – overlooking the Tower of London. London's oldest church, it was established in 675 by the Saxon Abbey at Barking and for many years was (confusingly) named after the abbey, All Hallows Barking.

The church was expanded and rebuilt several times and its location by the Tower saw the beheaded victims of executions (including Thomas More) buried there temporarily. The church survived the Great Fire of 1666 but suffered extensive bomb damage during the Second World War. There's an excellent café next door.

All Hallows by the Tower, Byward St, EC3R 5BJ (020-7481 2928; www.ahbtt.org.uk; Tower Hill tube; Mon-Fri 8am-6pm, Sat-Sun 10am-5pm).

Brompton Oratory

The Church of the Immaculate Heart of Mary – popularly known as the Brompton/London Oratory – is a stunning Roman Catholic church on Brompton Road, next to the Victoria and Albert Museum. It's the church of a community of priests (lay brothers) called The Congregation of the Oratory of St Philip Neri or Oratorians, founded by Neri (1515-1595) in Rome.

The Oratory was designed by Herbert Gribble, who won a competition for the job at the age of just 28, and the unabashed Italian style and ebullient design are entirely intentional. The result is a ravishing church that's unique in Britain, particularly in its use of decorative colour and structure.

Brompton Oratory, Brompton Rd, SW7 2RP (020-7808 0900; www.bromptonoratory.co.uk; S Kensington tube; daily 6am-8pm; tours can be arranged).

Christ Church Spitalfields

The lovely 18th-century Christ Church Spitalfields is located in East London and was designed by Nicholas Hawksmoor (1661-1736), a pupil of Sir Christopher Wren and one of England's foremost architects. It was built between 1714 and 1729 and is noted for the eloquence of its beautiful stonework, pleasing geometry and proportions; the church is the size of a small cathedral and inside is the height of Exeter Cathedral with a volume half that of the nave of St Paul's.

Just as Christ Church is the masterpiece of its architect, the organ installed in 1735 was considered the greatest work of Georgian England's best organ builder, Richard Bridge (d. 1758).

Christ Church Spitalfields, Commercial St, E1 6LY (020-7377 6793; www. christchurchspitalfields.org and www. ccspitalfields.org; Liverpool St tube/rail or Aldgate E tube; Mon-Fri 10am-4pm, Sun 1-4pm).

Holy Trinity Sloane Square

This ravishing Victorian Anglican parish church was designed by John Dando Sedding (1836-1891) and built in 1888-90 in a striking Arts and Crafts style – it's aptly dubbed the 'Cathedral of the Arts and Crafts movement'. Grade I listed, Holy Trinity Sloane Square was certainly conceived on a grand scale; it's the widest church in the capital, eclipsing even St Paul's Cathedral by nine inches.

However, it's the internal fittings that make Holy Trinity stand out as one of the finest Victorian churches in England, featuring the work of leading sculptors and designers of the day, including F. W. Pomeroy, H. H. Armstead, Onslow Ford and Hamo Thornycroft.

Holy Trinity Sloane Square, Sloane St, SW1X 9BZ (020-7730 7270; www. holytrinitysloanesquare.co.uk; Sloane Sq tube; daily from around 7.30am-6pm – check before travelling).

King's College Chapel

King's College Chapel (Grade I listed) is a magnificent example of Victorian architecture, designed by the eminent architect George Gilbert Scott (1811-1878) on the lines of an ancient Christian basilica and completed in 1864. The beautiful Scott chapel is situated on the first floor directly above the Great Hall, reached by an impressive double staircase from the main entrance.

Among the many highlights are the organ by Henry Willis, dating from the 1860s, reconstructed by his grandson in the '30s; the lovely angel designs on the largest pipes were only revealed during restoration in 2000-01. The chapel also houses a wealth of poignant memorials.

King's College Chapel, King's College, Strand, WC2R 2LS (020-7836 5454; www.kcl. ac.uk/aboutkings/principal/dean/chaplaincy/ prayeratkings/strand/college-chapel.aspx; Temple tube; see website for opening hours and service times).

Methodist Central Hall, Westminster

Methodist Central Hall – also called Westminster Central Hall – is a magnificent, richly-decorated Methodist church designed by Edwin Alfred Rickards (1872-1920) in Viennese Baroque style with Romanesque decoration. It was built in 1905-11 to mark the centenary of the death of John Wesley (the founder of Methodism) in 1791 and was funded by the 'Wesleyan Methodist Twentieth Century Fund' – or the 'Million Guinea Fund' as it became known – which raised one million guineas from one million Methodists.

The beautiful Great Hall – with its impressive domed ceiling – seats up to 2,160 people and houses a splendid organ with 4,731 pipes.

Methodist Central Hall, Storey's Gate, SW1H 9NH (020-7654 3809; http://methodist-central-hall.org. uk; Westminster/St James's Pk tube; open daily, free guided tours between 9.30am and 5pm).

Neasden Temple

Included in the *Readers Digest* list of the 'Seventy Wonders of the Modern World', the BAPS Shri Swaminarayan Mandir, London (popularly known as the Neasden Temple) is a place of worship and prayer for Hindus.

The magnificent Temple is the largest of its kind outside India – its assembly hall can accommodate 5,000 people – 70ft high, covering 1.5 acres and topped by several pinnacles and five domes: it rises like an otherworldly wedding cake silhouetted against the capital's skyline. Its construction took just two years but consumed some 3,000 tons of the finest Bulgarian limestone and 2,000 tons of Italian Carrara marble, all hand-carved in India into 26,300 pieces and shipped to London for assembly.

BAPS Shri Swaminarayan Mandir, 105-119 Brentfield Rd, Neasden, NW10 8LD (020-8965 2651; http://londonmandir.baps.org; Neasden tube; daily 9am-6pm).

St Bartholomew the Great

Named for one of the 12 Apostles, this is one of London's oldest churches, with a rich history and interesting architecture and interior features, but Great St Bart's (as it's

sometimes called) is surprisingly little known. A priory church was first established here in 1123 as part of a monastery of Augustinian canons and the site has been in continuous use as a place of worship since at least 1143. The Grade I listed church survived the Great Fire and the Second World War, and boasts London's most significant Norman interior, with massive pillars, Romanesque arches and zig-zag moulding.

The excellent Cloister Café is open daily.

St Bartholomew the Great, W Smithfield, EC1A 9DS (020-7606 5171; www.greatstbarts.com; Barbican tube; see website for seasonal opening hours; adults £5, concessions £4.50, families £12).

St Bride's Church

St Bride's is built on a site used by the Romans and is one of London's oldest church sites, probably dating to a Middle Saxon conversion in the 7th century, and perhaps even founded by  St Bridget in the 6th century. The current church is the eighth on the site and was built by Sir Christopher Wren from 1672 to replace the 11th-century Norman church destroyed in the Great Fire in 1666.

Set back from Fleet Street, St Bride's (Grade I listed) – known appropriately as the 'Journalists' Church' – is a striking sight, with Wren's tallest (tiered) spire at 226ft, which is said to have inspired the shape of modern wedding cakes.

St Bride's Church, Fleet St, EC4Y 8AU (020-7427 0133; www.stbrides.com; St Paul's tube; Mon-Fri 8am-6pm, Sat hours vary, Sun 10am-6.30pm).

St James's Church

A majestic Anglican parish church on Piccadilly, St James's (Grade I listed) was designed by Sir Christopher Wren and consecrated in 1684. It's considered the finest of a group of four similar churches that Wren designed on large open sites, which he singled out for special praise. The beautiful interior boasts a number of superb features, including a carved marble font and limewood reredos by Grinling Gibbons. The church was badly damaged during the Second World War, after which the 'secret' Southwood Garden was created as a garden of remembrance and a venue for outdoor sculpture exhibitions.

The church also has an impressive music programme, and hosts various markets (see website) and a café.

St James's Church, 197 Piccadilly, W1J 9LL (020-7734 4511; www.sjp. org.uk; Piccadilly Circus tube; daily 8am-6.30pm).

St Margaret's Church

Standing between Westminster Abbey and the Houses of Parliament, the original St Margaret's (dedicated to St Margaret of Antioch) was thought to have been built in the latter part of the 11th century. It was rebuilt between 1482 and 1523 and there were further restorations in the 18th-20th centuries, although the structure remains essentially the same; the interior was restored and altered by Sir George Gilbert Scott in 1877.

St Margaret's became the parish church of the Palace of Westminster in 1614, when Parliamentary services were first held here; the connection continues to this day and has led St Margaret's to be dubbed 'the parish church of the House of Commons.'

St Margaret's Church, St Margaret St, SW1P 3JX (020-7654 4840; www.westminster-abbey.org/st-margarets; Westminster tube; Mon-Fri 9.30am-3.30pm, Sat 9.30am-1.30pm, Sun 2-4.30pm).

St Martin-in-the-Fields

St Martin-in-the-Fields (Grade I listed) is one of London's most beloved non-cathedral churches, noted for its fine architecture, musical tradition and work with the poor. It's an Anglican church dedicated to

St Martin of Tours (316-397), a Bishop whose shrine became a famous stop-over for pilgrims on the road to Santiago de Compostela. The church was rebuilt by Henry VIII in 1542 to keep plague victims from being taken through his Palace of Whitehall, although the iconic (much copied) building you see today was designed by James Gibbs and completed in 1726.

The church is famous for its lunchtime and evening concerts, and the crypt houses a popular, award-winning café.

St Martin-in-the-Fields, Trafalgar Sq, WC2N 4JH (020-7766 1100; www. stmartin-in-the-fields. org; Charing Cross/ Embankment tube; see website for opening times).

St Paul's Cathedral

An Anglican cathedral and the seat of the Bishop of London, St Paul's is the City's most iconic building. It sits atop the highest hill (Ludgate) and at 365ft (111m) it was, until 1962, the tallest structure in London – its dome still dominates the skyline. Designed by Sir Christopher Wren, the English Baroque masterpiece is the fifth church to stand here – the first dated from 604AD – and was built between 1675 and 1710 after its predecessor was destroyed in the Great Fire of London.

Tours of St Paul's Cathedral take in its magnificent interior, the galleries that wind around its dome, its chapels and crypt. The Golden Gallery encircles the highest point of St Paul's dome, providing panoramic views across the City and River Thames. It's well worth climbing the 528 steps, but if you cannot manage it Oculus (see below) can take you there.

The crypt is the largest in Europe and is the last resting place of some of the nation's greatest heroes, poets and scientists including Sir Christopher Wren, the Duke of Wellington and Lord Nelson, whose black marble sarcophagus has centre stage directly beneath the dome. The former Treasury in the crypt hosts Oculus, a 270° film experience that tells the 1,400-year history of the church; it takes you on a virtual tour of the building and flies you through Wren's Great Model, the room-sized model he built for Charles II.

The Cathedral also has a bookshop, café and restaurant.

St Paul's Cathedral, St Paul's Churchyard, EC4M 8AD (020-7246 8350; www.stpauls. co.uk; St Paul's tube; Mon-Sat 8.30am-4pm; see website for fees).

St Paul's Church

Commonly known as 'The Actors' Church', St Paul's in Covent Garden is a beautiful parish church with an impressive Tuscan portico. It was designed by Inigo Jones in 1631 (completed in 1633) as part of a commission by Francis Russell, 4th Earl of Bedford, to create a square with 'houses and buildings fit for the habitations of gentlemen and men of ability'.

The church contains a wealth of memorials dedicated to famous personalities including Charlie Chaplin, Noel Coward, Gracie Fields, Stanley Holloway, Boris Karloff, Vivien Leigh and Ivor Novello. The artist J.M.W. Turner and dramatist W.S. Gilbert (of Gilbert and Sullivan fame) were both baptised at St Paul's.

St Paul's Church, 31 Bedford St, WC2E 9ED (020-7836 5221; www.actorschurch.org; Covent Gdn tube; Mon-Fri 8.30am-5pm, Sat varies, Sun 9am-1pm).

St Stephen Walbrook

This elegant City church has a long history, dating back at least to the time of the Romans. In the 2nd century AD a temple of Mithras stood on the bank of the River Walbrook, a stream running across London from the City Wall near Moorfields to the Thames. The church that replaced it may date back to 700 AD.

The current church was built by Sir Christopher Wren between 1672 and 1680 and is considered to be one of Wren's finest church interiors – if not *the* finest. The influential German-born British scholar of art and architecture Sir Nikolaus Pevsner declared it one of England's ten most important buildings, so it certainly merits attention.

St Stephen Walbrook, 39 Walbrook, EC4N 8BN (020-7626 9000; www.ststephenwalbrook.net; Bank tube; see website for visiting hours).

Southwark Cathedral

Often overlooked in a much-visited part of London (the buzzy south bank of the Thames, near London Bridge and Borough Market), Southwark Cathedral is both beautiful and historic. It has been a place of worship for over 1,000 years and is the mother church of the Anglican diocese of Southwark, although it has only been designated a cathedral since 1905. It's strategically sited at the oldest crossing point of the tidal Thames and has long been a place not just of worship but also of hospitality and refuge.

There are unsubstantiated claims that a convent was founded on the site in 606AD followed by a monastery established in the 9th century by St Swithun, although the site's first official mention is in the *Domesday Book* of 1086, as the 'minster' of Southwark. The current building is mainly Gothic, dating from 1220 to 1420, making it London's first Gothic church. A Norman arch from the 12th century survives in the north aisle of the nave and there's an oak effigy of a knight dating from around 1275, plus a wealth of memorials.

The churchyard is a tranquil haven at the heart of London and a favourite lunch spot for visitors and the area's office workers. The Cathedral is also a popular venue for concerts and recitals – see the website for the programme of events.

Southwark Cathedral, London Bridge, SE1 9DA (020-7367 6700; http://cathedral.southwark. anglican.org; London Br tube/rail; Mon-Fri 8am-6pm, Sat-Sun 8.30am-6pm).

Temple Church

At the heart of legal London sits the Temple Church (1185), one of London's most striking and historic churches, built by the Knights Templar or Red Knights in the 12th century. With some 800 years of unbroken history – from the Crusaders through the turmoil of the Reformation, Civil War, Great Fire and Second World War bombs – it has survived virtually intact.

The church was rented to two colleges of lawyers which evolved into the Inner and Middle Temples, two of the four Inns of Court (see page 33). Today it's held in common by both Inns and is the main chapel of those who work in the Temple.

Temple Church, Temple, EC4Y 7BB (020-7353 3470; www.templechurch.com; Temple tube; see website for opening times; adults £5, concessions £3, 16s and under free).

Tyburn Convent

Founded in 1901, Tyburn Convent is dedicated to the Roman Catholic martyrs who were hanged at the nearby Tyburn Tree gallows (and elsewhere) for espousing their Catholic faith during the Reformation (1535-1681). In the convent's crypt you can see some gruesome relics of the Catholic martyrs' executions, including

bloodstained clothing, fingernails, bone fragments and locks of hair, which are preserved in the cold, dry cellar.

The convent is a cloistered community of some 25 Benedictine contemplatives, who never leave their enclosed walls except for medical treatment. It's a surprising, peaceful and welcoming sanctuary among the surrounding noise and chaos of the West End.

Tyburn Convent, 8 Hyde Park Pl, W2 2LJ (020-7723 7262; www.tyburnconvent.org.uk; Marble Arch tube; tours of the shrine and crypt daily at 10.30am, 3.30pm and 5.30pm).

Westminster Abbey

Westminster Abbey is steeped in over a thousand years of history. Benedictine monks first came to the site in the middle of the 10th century, establishing a tradition of daily worship that continues to this day. The Abbey also has a strong royal connection; it's where many British monarchs have been crowned, married and laid to rest. The present church was begun by Henry III in 1245, and is one of the most important Gothic buildings in the country, with the medieval shrine of an Anglo-Saxon saint at its heart.

An architectural masterpiece of the 13th to 16th centuries, the Abbey presents a unique pageant of British history: the shrine of St Edward the Confessor, the tombs of 17 kings and queens, and countless memorials to the famous and the great. It has been the setting for every Coronation since 1066 and numerous other royal occasions, including 16 royal weddings. Today it remains a church dedicated to regular worship and to the celebration of great events in the life of the nation. There are also a number of lovely gardens.

Neither a cathedral nor a parish church, Westminster Abbey (or the Collegiate Church of St Peter Westminster, to give it its correct title) is a 'Royal Peculiar' under the jurisdiction of a Dean and Chapter, subject only to the Sovereign and not to any archbishop or bishop.

Westminster Abbey, 20 Deans Yd, SW1P 3PA (020-7222 5152; www.westminster-abbey.org; Westminster tube; see website for visiting times and fees; free entry to gardens).

Westminster Cathedral

Not to be confused with Westminster Abbey (the mother church of the Church of England), Westminster Cathedral is the largest Catholic church in England and Wales, and the mother church of the English and Welsh Catholic community. Unlike the Abbey, it's a relatively modern building; construction began in 1895 and it opened in 1903.

The Cathedral isn't a conventional late-Victorian building, but is modelled on a Byzantine basilica, made of brick, with the interior decorated with marble and mosaics. The outside resembles a wedding cake, with pseudo-Byzantine copper domes and a terracotta bell tower with white Portland stone stripes. The bell tower rises elegantly to 273 feet with a viewing gallery at 210 feet commanding spectacular views.

The interior of the Cathedral contains fine marble work and exotic mosaics (with gold and shades of blue), while the majestic 14

Stations of the Cross are represented by carved limestone panels by sculptor Eric Gill (1882-1940). Some 126 different varieties of marble from 24 countries on five continents decorate the Cathedral, probably more than in any other building in England.

As a final bonus, Westminster Cathedral has a splendid choir – one of the country's best – that sings mass most evenings, providing an atmospheric free concert.

Westminster Cathedral, 42 Francis St, SW1P 1QW (020-7798 9055; www. westminstercathedral.org.uk; Victoria tube/rail; Mon-Fri 8am-7pm, Sat-Sun 10am-1pm).

14.
Pubs

British pubs (public houses) are world renowned for their unique atmosphere, bonhomie and fine beer, while increasing numbers are also noted for their excellent cuisine. Nowhere is this diversity and quality more evident than in London, which has a bewildering variety of watering holes: classic historic boozers, traditional riverside inns, specialist craft beer pubs, mouth-watering gastropubs, arty theatre pubs and more...

Pubs that specialise in high-quality food are often referred to as 'gastropubs' – a combination of the French word gastronomique and pub – although not all pubs that serve good food make this claim and some that do fail to live up to it. Most gastropubs have a dining room for diners (booking advisable, if not essential) and a bar for drinkers, although you can usually eat in the bar as well. While the concept of a restaurant in a pub has reinvigorated both pub culture and dining out, it has also attracted criticism for altering the essential character of traditional pubs. However, the best gastropubs are 'proper' pubs, serving craft beers in a 'pubby' atmosphere alongside gourmet food and fine wines.

This chapter includes 20 of our favourite London pubs in all corners of the city, each with something to commend it – from stunning Victorian décor and floorboards steeped in history to brilliant beers and the warmest of welcomes. Cheers!

The Anchor & Hope

Close to the Young Vic theatre, the Anchor & Hope is one of London's best-known gastropubs. It's a no-frills venue, with minimal decor, bare wooden tables and art to brighten the walls, while the menu is chalked on a board. The food is tasty, modern British fare, served in hearty portions and reasonably priced – the 'worker's lunch' is especially good value.

The Anchor is generally busy and the 'no reservations' policy (except for Sunday lunch) means that you may have to wait for a table, although you can relax in the bar and enjoy something from the comprehensive wine list, which includes a reasonable choice by the glass.

The Anchor & Hope, 36 The Cut, SE1 8LP (020-7928 9898; www.anchorandhopepub.co.uk; Southwark rail; Mon 5-11pm, Tue-Sat 11am-11pm, Sun 12.30-3.15pm).

The Black Friar

The wedge-shaped, Grade II listed Black Friar has an attractive exterior, but inside it's nothing less than spectacular. The elaborate and sumptuous decoration is a blend of Arts and Crafts and Art Nouveau styles, the latter a rarity in London. The building dates from 1875 and is on the site of a medieval Dominican Friary, which is reflected in the decoration: friars feature everywhere in the pub's cascade of intricate friezes, mosaics, reliefs and sculptures.

It's a Nicholson's pub with an impressive range of ales, including guest beers, plus reasonably-priced wine and good pub food. Regulars prefer to escape the hubbub by drinking outside, where the seating area is unusually generous for the cramped City.

The Black Friar, 174 Queen Victoria St, EC4V 4EG (020-7236 5474; www.nicholsonspubs. co.uk/theblackfriarblackfriarslondon; Blackfriars tube/rail; Mon-Sat 9am-11pm, Sun noon-10.30pm).

The Chapel

One of London's earliest gastropubs, the Chapel has won many awards since opening in 1995. Its interior is typical of the genre – light and airy with wooden floors – but

it also boasts a walled garden and terrace, a rare bonus for a central London pub. There's a choice of menus – including antipasti and canapés if you want a lighter bite (see website) – with main dishes including the likes of griddled wild sea trout, confit duck leg and seven-hour Swaledale lamb shoulder.

There's also a comprehensive and fairly-priced wine list and a good choice of ales, including Adnams and IPA on draught.

The Chapel, 48 Chapel St, NW1 5DP (020-7402 9220; http://thechapellondon.com; Edgware Rd tube; Mon-Sat noon-11pm, Sun noon-10.30pm).

The Cittie of York

This Sam Smith's establishment looks as if it could be one of London's oldest pubs; a sign outside states that there's been a tavern here since 1430. However, the current one is a rebuild dating from 1924 and the pub has only been known by its current Olde English-sounding name since 1979.

Despite the somewhat faux antiquity, the Cittie of York is Grade II listed, and is an impressive space, a large, warren-like pub with more than a hint of baronial hall about it. There's a vaulted ceiling, a notably long bar and numerous side booths, originally designed for lawyers to have undisturbed chats (and refreshments) with their clients – this part of town is London's legal heartland.

The Cittie of York, 22 High Holborn, WC1V 6BN (020-7242 7670; Chancery Lane/Holborn tube; Mon-Sat noon-11pm, closed Sun).

The Eagle

This trail-blazing local on Farringdon Road was arguably the UK's first-ever gastropub. It started serving posh pub grub in 1991 and has stayed true to its principles while many imitators have fallen by the wayside. The Eagle does the gastropub 'model' perfectly, offering a good pint or glass of wine with well-cooked food at reasonable prices in a pared-back, unembellished space, with large windows providing plenty of natural light.

Around six beers are available (including real ales) and there's a short wine list and even a few cocktails. The menu is chalked on blackboards and consists mainly of well-executed Mediterranean fare cooked in an open kitchen. Typical dishes may include *pappa al pomodoro* (Tuscan bread and tomato 'porridge'); linguine with clams; braised peas, jamón and aioli; and pan-fried scallops with chorizo on toast. The superb steak sandwiches are also hard to resist.

Friendly, efficient staff oversee proceedings and while it isn't a venue for an intimate date – it can be crowded and noisy, with some shared tables – the Eagle has a great vibe. There's no booking, so arrive early or late to ensure a seat.

The Eagle, 159 Farringdon Rd, EC1R 3AL (020-7837 1353; www.theeaglefarringdon.co.uk; Farringdon tube/rail; Mon-Sat noon-11pm, Sun noon-5pm).

The George Inn

One of London's most famous pubs, the George is the city's only remaining galleried coaching inn, Grade I listed and worth visiting for its history alone. There's been a hostelry here since 1598 – probably much earlier – but the current structure dates from 1676, when the inn was rebuilt after a fire destroyed much of Southwark. It's no longer complete, but enough remains to give you a good idea of what such inns were like.

Shakespeare, Pepys and Johnson reputedly drank at the George, and Charles Dickens mentions it in *Little Dorrit*. These days, it's owned by the National Trust and on the tourist trail and therefore usually busy, although there are plenty of tables in the large courtyard.

The George Inn, 75-77 Borough High St, SE1 1NH (020-7407 2056; www.george-southwark. co.uk; London Bridge tube/rail; Mon-Sat 11am-11pm, Sun noon-10.30pm).

The Guildford Arms

Food is the focus at the Guildford Arms, a friendly gastropub, with an elegant restaurant, a private dining room and a sunken garden, housed in a handsome Georgian building in Greenwich. The ground floor bar is relaxed and informal, offering a good selection of cask beers, lagers and wines, along with a bar menu featuring light bites, seasonal dishes and pub classics. Upstairs, the fine-dining restaurant is where chef-proprietor Guy Awford presents his modern British menu, showcasing the best of local and seasonal produce.

The spectacular sunken garden features both lawn and decked terrace areas, where white birch, grasses and kitchen herbs combine to create an oasis of calm.

The Guildford Arms, 55 Guildford Grove, SE10 8JY (020-8691 6293; www.theguildfordarms. co.uk; Deptford Br DLR; see website for opening times, closed Mon).

The Gun

Housed in a striking (Grade II listed) 18th-century building, the Gun overlooks the Thames in Docklands, just a short walk from Canary Wharf. For many years it was a run-down boozer for local foundry and river workers; Horatio Nelson was said to be a regular patron and allegedly enjoyed assignations with Lady Emma Hamilton in an upstairs room. After a fire in 2001 it was given a makeover by brothers Tom and Ed Martin, and is now a celebrated gastropub.

The Gun serves award-winning modern British cuisine, including such delights as pheasant, oysters and salt-marsh lamb. Most main courses are priced between £15 and £30 – prices more in tune with City traders than dockers – although bar grub is relatively affordable. In summer an alfresco bar serves Portuguese classics from a barbecue. There's a good choice of beer, with the likes of London Pride and Adnams ales as regulars, plus an extensive wine list.

High-backed leather armchairs, smartly turned-out waiters and panoramic views across the river from the large terrace are additional draws for this popular venue, where booking is recommended.

The Gun, 27 Coldharbour, E14 9NS (020-7515 5222; www.thegundocklands.com; Canary Wharf DLR; Mon-Sat 11.30am-midnight, Sun 11.30am-11pm).

The Harp

Built in the 1830s (and originally called the Welsh Harp), this centrally-located free house has an attractive stained-glass front and what's reputed to be the West End's best choice of real ale. It's an ever-changing selection, with regulars including Dark Star, Harveys, Sambrook's and Twickenham Ales.

The surrounds of the long, narrow bar counter are decorated with a large collection of beer mats, which is appropriate for a pub that was the first London boozer to win CAMRA's (Campaign for Real Ale) 'National Pub of the Year' award. Some wine is also sold, as is cider and perry (pear cider) – indeed, the Harp is a former winner of 'London Cider Pub of the Year'.

The Harp, 47 Chandos Pl, WC2N 4HS (020-7836 0291; www.harpcoventgarden.com; Charing Cross tube/rail; Mon-Thu 10.30am-11.30pm, Fri-Sat 10.30am-midnight, Sun noon-10.30pm).

The Holborn Whippet

A relatively recent arrival, the Holborn Whippet is a strangely-shaped corner bar in Sicilian Avenue, a small, stylish Edwardian shopping arcade. It's so named because 'the folk of Bloomsbury and Holborn parishes relaxed with a spot of whippet racing well into the 1800s'. The décor has hints of the '50s, with wooden floorboards, brown tiles, cream walls and pictures of dogs on the walls. Large windows provide fine views of the arcade, while there are outside tables for alfresco drinking in clement weather.

While there's a constantly changing wine list and good sandwiches, posh burgers and pizza, craft beer is the main attraction with at least 15 beers on tap.

The Holborn Whippet, 25-29 Sicilian Ave, WC1A 2QH (020-3137 9937; www.holbornwhippet. com; Holborn tube; Mon-Sat noon-11.30pm, Sun noon-10.30pm).

The Junction Tavern

A large corner establishment with an enviable reputation, the Junction Tavern caters equally to both gourmets and beer aficionados. It's a typical Victorian affair with high ceilings and elaborately carved dark wood, and a choice of places to sit, including the warm and friendly front bar area – with a stunning bar top and original fireplace – an airy conservatory, large heated garden terrace and award-winning beer garden.

The daily changing menu is modern British bistro, while weekend options include Saturday brunch and all-day Sunday lunch. There's a reasonably-priced and comprehensive wine list, with many available by the glass, plus a good choice of ales.

The Junction Tavern, 101 Fortess Rd, NW5 1AG (020-7485 9400; junctiontavern.co.uk; Tufnell Pk tube or Kentish Town tube/rail; Mon-Thu 5-11pm, Fri-Sat noon-midnight, Sun noon-11pm).

The Ladbroke Arms

A free house on a tranquil street in Holland Park, the Ladbroke Arms is a destination pub for both foodies and drinkers, attracted by its eye-catching exterior, welcoming vibe, tasty food, good beer and extensive wine list. In summer the pub is festooned with an award-winning display of hanging baskets, while inside the look is pure gastropub: light and airy with wooden floors and a pretty terrace for sunny days.

The eclectic menu takes inspiration from around the globe, using fresh ingredients to produce tasty dishes such as linguine nero with octopus, clams, chilli and white wine, and beef cheek stew with roast vegetables.

The Ladbroke Arms, 54 Ladbroke Rd, W11 3NW (020-7727 6648; www.ladbrokearms.com; Holland Pk tube; Mon-Sat 11.30am-11pm, Sun noon-10.30pm).

The Mall Tavern

The Mall Tavern is a large, handsome Victorian corner pub in Notting Hill with a striking central bar (complete with chandeliers), a lovely walled garden, three private dining spaces and a 'secret' diners' club. It's owned by the Perritt brothers who in 2010 transformed what was then a run-down boozer into a modern local with great food and charming service, while still managing to retain the atmosphere of a 'real' pub.

and butter beans or Jacob's Ladder beef rib with slaw. If you've room left for dessert try the scrummy apple and cinnamon crumble with Calvados custard or dark chocolate mousse with shortbread biscuits.

Drinkers aren't neglected, with three changing cask ales (such as Otter Bitter, Sambrook's Wandle and Sharp's Doom Bar), craft ciders, a classic cocktail list and some 30 wines.

The Mall Tavern, 71 Palace Gardens Ter, W8 4RU (020-7229 3374; www.themallw8.com; Notting Hill Gate tube; Mon-Sat noon-midnight, Sun noon-10.30pm).

The menu is the creation of Jesse Dunford Wood, a master of modern British food (with a twist) and sometime celebrity chef, having appeared on BBC's *Masterchef* and *The Truth about Food*. His food is imaginative and moreish. Typical starters may include duck & cognac rillettes with pear chutney or 'Freemans' spinach, artichoke and cream cheese dip, followed by mains of baked cod, salsify, chanterelles

Paradise by Way of Kensal Green

The marvellously named Paradise by Way of Kensal Green is a charming, bohemian combination of pub, restaurant and party venue, consisting of a rabbit warren of intimate and larger spaces decorated in eclectic, shabby-chic style. The modern British menu includes treats such as Morecambe Bay shrimps, Lonk lamb and Dorset lobster, plus delicious Sunday roasts.

With its bizarre, banquet-sized dining room – containing a melange of antiques, mirrors and chandeliers – a lovely courtyard garden and decked roof terrace, the über-stylish Paradise is well named. It's also one of the city's most fashionable party spots with a variety of private function rooms.

Paradise by Way of Kensal Green, 19 Kilburn Ln, W10 4AE (020-8969 0098; www.theparadise. co.uk; Ladbroke Grove tube; Mon-Wed 4pm-midnight, Thu 4pm-1am, Fri 4pm-2am, Sat noon-2am, Sun noon-11.30pm).

The Peasant

Midway between Smithfield and the Angel, the Peasant was one of London's pioneering gastropubs and is still pulling in the punters. It's an imposing Victorian public house – an inviting, light and airy place – with arched windows, huge mirrors, a horseshoe-shaped bar and an old mosaic floor thought to date from the 17th century. There's a broad choice of bar food – from sharing plates, such as ploughman's or Mediterranean mezze, to roast meats and comfort puddings – while the upstairs restaurant serves an imaginative set menu.

The Peasant also appeals to serious drinkers, with an ever-changing choice of real ales, lagers, ciders and around 50 wines. Children and dogs are welcome. Booking is recommended.

The Peasant, 240 St John St, EC1V 4PH (020-7336 7726; www.thepeasant.co.uk; Farringdon tube/rail; Mon-Sat noon-11pm, Sun noon-10.30pm).

The Princess Louise

Built in 1872 and named after one of Queen Victoria's daughters, this Sam Smith's establishment is one of London's best-preserved Victorian pubs. Though it's unremarkable from the outside, the interior is a riot of mosaic tiles, etched glass, moulded ceilings, mirrors and carved wood, a fine tribute to Victorian

craftsmanship. Such ostentation was once common in English pub interiors, perhaps a reflection of the confidence and wealth of a country with the world's largest empire.

In addition to the regulars from nearby Bloomsbury's educational and cultural establishments, the Princess Louise attracts a steady stream of tourists, its glorious glitz having earned it a place in many guidebooks.

The Princess Louise, 208 High Holborn, WC1V 7EP (020-7405 8816; http://princesslouisepub. co.uk; Holborn tube; Mon-Fri 11am-11pm, Sat noon-11pm, Sun noon-6.45pm).

The Princess of Shoreditch

The acclaimed Princess of Shoreditch is a handsome award-winning gastropub occupying a lovely light-filled 270-year-old building with a spiral staircase linking the downstairs bar and the upstairs dining room. It's a proper pub with a good choice of real ales and an interesting wine list, but the big attraction is the food.

The Princess is big on provenance and sources its venison, game birds and delicious beef from Chart Farm in Kent (the lamb is also from Kent),

pork from Kilravock Farm in Nairnshire (Scotland) and sustainable fish from day boats on the south coast. Quality fare cooked to perfection in gorgeous surroundings.

The Princess of Shoreditch, 76-78 Paul St, EC2A 4NE (020-7729 9270; www. theprincessofshoreditch.com; Old St tube; Mon-Sat noon-11pm, Sun noon-10.30pm).

The Wells

A short walk from Hampstead Heath, the Wells dates back to the early 18th century when Hampstead was the location of several spas (or wells). A run-down boozer rescued in 2003, it has been transformed into an acclaimed 'pub-with-food' and is a highlight of the Hampstead gastro scene. Some original Georgian features remain, which are combined with modern decorative touches to make for an eye-catching venue.

A diverse menu offers both lunch and dinner, plus roasts on Sundays. Sample starters include fig, gorgonzola and prosciutto salad or ham hock terrine; mains range from pan-fried Icelandic cod with crispy globe artichoke and romesco sauce, to venison meatballs with linguini and chilli ragu. If you have room for a pud you can dig into passion fruit Pavlova or a dark chocolate pot. Prices are at the top end for gastro fare, but not excessive for food of this quality.

The wine list is well considered, categorised by character rather than grape (a few are available by the glass), while beer drinkers can enjoy solid favourites such as London Pride and Black Sheep. Dogs are welcome and there are even snacks for your four-legged friend!

The Wells, 30 Well Walk, NW3 1BX (020-7794 3785; http://thewellshampstead.london; Hampstead tube; Mon-Sat noon-11pm, Sun noon-10.30pm).

The White Horse

The White Horse (aka 'The Sloaney Pony'), a lovely historic pub overlooking Parsons Green, is a magnet for both foodies and beer lovers. There's been a coaching inn on the site since at least 1688, but the current building is a haven of Victorian elegance with a pleasing blend of traditional polished mahogany wall panels, wood and flagstone floors, large windows, open fires and contemporary lighting.

The White Horse manages to be both one of the UK's best beer pubs – with an unrivalled choice of cask and bottled beers from around the globe – and a serious foodie destination. Not cheap but good value for this neck of the woods.

The White Horse, 1-3 Parsons Grn, SW6 4UL (020-7736 2115; www.whitehorsesw6.com; Parsons Grn tube; Sun-Wed 9.30am-11.30pm, Thu-Sat 9.30am-midnight).

Ye Olde Cheshire Cheese

One of the City's must-see pubs, Ye Olde Cheshire Cheese was already a century and a half old when it was rebuilt in 1667 after the previous year's Great Fire. Its vaulted cellars are even older, and are thought to have belonged to a 13th-century Carmelite monastery. Today, it's an attractive creaky warren of bars, especially atmospheric in winter when there's a cosy coal fire. It feels like a genuine history trip, and perhaps the long list of noted regulars and visitors (including Dr Johnson and Charles Dickens) has left its mark.

The Cheese is a Sam Smith's pub, offering the brewery's usual range of well-priced ales and traditional pub fare.

Ye Olde Cheshire Cheese, 145 Fleet St, EC4A 2BU (020-7353 6170; Chancery Lane/Temple tube; Mon-Fri 11.30am-11pm, Sat noon-11pm, closed Sun).

15.
Shops

The British are a nation of diehard shoppers and retail therapy is an all-consuming passion and the country's favourite leisure activity – and London is its beating heart. It's one of the world's most exciting shopping cities, packed with grand department stores, trend-setting boutiques, traditional traders, edgy concept stores, absorbing antiques' emporiums, eccentric novelty shops, exclusive purveyors of luxury goods, mouth-watering food halls, bustling markets and much more.

Not surprisingly, vast shopping centres, ubiquitous chain stores and supermarkets abound, yet small independent shops manage to survive (and even flourish) and are the lifeblood of the city. Despite increasing competition, particularly from online shopping, and the ever-present shadow of recession, London's independent shopping scene goes from strength to strength, and is constantly reinventing itself to meet the challenges of the 21st century. Our selection of the city's best retailers includes shops with glorious interiors, original wares, unique atmospheres, unmatchable variety and outstanding customer service.

Whether you wish to revitalise your wardrobe or restock your larder, buy a new computer or an antique chair, track down a designer watch or a rare first edition – or find a gift for someone who's impossible to buy for – you're bound to find inspiration in London.

Daunt Books

Founded in 1990 by James Daunt, the Daunt flagship store on Marylebone High Street is housed in a beautiful Edwardian building dating from 1912, believed to be the first custom-built bookshop in the world. The back room is particularly impressive, with its original oak mezzanine gallery, graceful skylights and stained-glass window. Entering Daunts is like being transported to a calmer, more graceful era, when people had time to browse and customer service wasn't just a cliché.

A specialist in travel titles, Daunt Books has only been trading for over 25 years – a relatively short time in the book world – but now has six shops and an enviable reputation as one of London's most treasured independent booksellers.

Daunt Books, 83 Marylebone High St, W1U 4QW (020-7224 2295; www.dauntbooks.co.uk; Baker St tube; Mon-Sat 9am-7.30pm, Sun 11am-6pm).

David Morris

Bespoke jeweller David Morris was established in 1962 and shot to fame a year later when Morris and his design partner were awarded the 9th De Beers Diamonds International Award in New York (they won it again in 1964). Now firmly established as one of London's (if not the world's) most esteemed jewellery brands, the enviable client list has included Queen Noor of Jordan, 'Queen' of Hollywood Elizabeth Taylor, Princess Margaret, Princess Anne and Diana, Princess of Wales.

The company is now managed by David's son, Jeremy – also the principal designer – who continues to design and craft dazzling couture jewellery of the very highest quality.

David Morris, 180 New Bond St, W1S 4RL (020-7499 2200; www.davidmorris.com; Green Pk tube; Mon-Fri 10am-6pm, Sat 10.30am-5pm, closed Sun).

Dover Street Market

A hip store with an industrial warehouse vibe, über-cool Dover Street Market was founded by Comme des Garçons designer Rei Kawakubo and offers a novel approach to clothes shopping: it's a quirky, design-led store with an edgy street-market feel. But don't let the 'market' tag fool you, as prices here aren't cheap. The store stocks rarefied labels such as Lanvin, Givenchy, Celine, Azzedine Alaïa and Rick Owens, alongside the complete Comme des Garçons range in a seemingly ad hoc, constantly evolving space. Don't let the name fool you either – DSM was originally based in Dover Street, Mayfair, until March 2016, when it moved to the Grade II listed former Burberry building on Haymarket.

The store offers an original take on consumerism that combines a constantly evolving market atmosphere with avant-garde design. The minimalist, functional interior – with shop fittings made from raw and reclaimed materials such as shipping containers – provides a suitably stark backdrop for the many fashion designers, who are encouraged to adapt the space to suit their collection, making for a dynamic and unique interior.

While here take time out to visit the Rose Bakery, a classy café owned by Rose Carrarini, founder of the Villandry café-restaurant chain.

Dover Street Market, 18-22 Haymarket, SW1Y 4DG (020-7518 0680; http://london. doverstreetmarket.com; Piccadilly Circus tube; Mon-Sat 11am-7pm, Sun noon-6pm).

Fenwick

Founded by John James Fenwick in 1882 in Newcastle-upon-Tyne (the city is still home to its HQ and flagship store), Fenwick is an independent chain of 11 department stores, including two in London (Bond Street and Brent Cross). Situated on the capital's most fashionable shopping street, the New Bond Street store opened in 1891, doubling in size in 1980 to become the shop we see today. It's home to five floors of luxury retail including designer clothing, homeware, bags, shoes, fashion, jewellery, perfume, cosmetics, cards, gifts and more.

There's also a range of beauty services including a spa, massage, facials, nail bar and hair salon, plus two restaurants and a bar.

Fenwick, 63 New Bond St, W1S 1RQ (020-7629 9161; www.fenwick.co.uk/stores/bond-street; Bond St tube; Mon-Sat 9.30am-8pm, Sun noon-6pm).

Forbidden Planet

Named after the 1956 feature film, Forbidden Planet is the world's largest and best-known science fiction, fantasy and cult entertainment retailer, and the largest UK stockist of comics and graphic novels. It began in 1978 as a small store in Denmark Street, Soho, and has traded from its London megastore since 2003.

The store specialises in selling action figures, books, comics (including DC, Marvel and manga), DVDs, video games, graphic novels, clothing and toys, and offers the best merchandise from the cream of cult movies and television, including *The Avengers*, *Batman*, *Breaking Bad*, *Doctor Who*, *Game of Thrones*, *Star Trek*, *Star Wars*, *Transformers* and many more.

Forbidden Planet, 179 Shaftesbury Ave, WC2H 8JR (020-7420 3666; https://forbiddenplanet. com; Tottenham Court Rd tube; Mon-Tue 10am-7pm, Wed, Fri-Sat 10am-7.30pm, Thu 10am-8pm, Sun noon-6pm).

Fortnum & Mason

Fortnum & Mason (usually referred to simply as 'Fortnums') on Piccadilly is one of Britain's oldest department stores, established in 1707 by William Fortnum and Hugh Mason. Founded as a grocery store, its reputation was built on supplying top-quality food, and its fame grew rapidly throughout the Victorian era. Over the years it has developed into a department store, selling homeware, beauty products, fashion accessories, jewellery, perfumes, menswear, luggage and writing accessories.

However, Fortnums' reputation rests largely on its food hall, which is situated on the lower ground and ground floors. There's also a celebrated tearoom and no fewer than five restaurants.

Fortnum & Mason, 181 Piccadilly, W1A 1ER (020-7734 8040; www.fortnumandmason.com; Green Pk/Piccadilly tube; Mon-Sat 9am-10pm, Sun noon-6pm).

Foyles

Founded in 1903 – and still run by the Foyle family – this world-famous bookseller opened its new flagship store in 2014 at 107 Charing Cross Road, a few doors along from the iconic rabbit warren of a store it had occupied for over a century. It's one of Europe's largest bookshops with 37,000ft^2 of retail space spread over four floors, four miles of shelves and over 200,000 titles. An impressive full-height central atrium and large windows fill the space with natural light.

Alongside books, there's a wide range of gifts and stationery, magazines, printed music, classical music CDs, classic DVDs, as well as Ray's Jazz (a specialist music store), a café and an auditorium.

Foyles, 107 Charing Cross Rd, WC2H 0DT (020-7437 5660; www.foyles.co.uk; Tottenham Court Rd tube; Mon-Sat 9.30am-9pm, Sun noon-6pm).

Harrods

Founded in 1834, Harrods in Knightsbridge is the world's most famous department store and a British institution, even though it's now owned by Qatar Holdings who paid £1.5 billion for it in 2010. It's also one of the world's largest stores, extending to 4.5 acres, with more than 1 million ft² (305,000m²) of retail space over seven floors divided into some 330 departments. Harrods is said to be able to provide anything a customer wants: its motto is *Omnia Omnibus Ubique* (All Things for All People Everywhere) and its clientele is decidedly upmarket.

Harrods astonishes and intrigues in equal measure with its first-class service, retail theatre and product quality, not to mention an unmatched international brand selection.

From its humble beginnings as a grocer it has become a Terracotta Palace crammed with luxury merchandise, from bags to beds, haute couture to homeware, pianos to pet accessories, plus a selection of premier services such as 'by appointment' personal shopping, Harrods bank and gold bullion.

Its pièce de résistance is its celebrated Art Nouveau food hall, where the majestic décor provides a glorious backdrop for the artful displays of food, notable for its variety, quality and luxury – and eye-watering prices! There are also some 30 restaurants and food outlets serving everything from frozen yogurt to oysters.

Harrods, 87-135 Brompton Rd, SW1X 7XL (020-7730 1234; www.harrods.com; Knightsbridge tube; Mon-Sat 10am-9pm, Sun noon-6pm).

Harvey Nichols

The younger, more fashionable cousin of Harrods, Harvey Nichols (dubbed 'Harvey Nicks') was founded in 1813 as a linen shop and has grown into a nationwide chain of prestigious department stores: its original flagship store is in Knightsbridge, with others in Birmingham, Bristol, Dublin, Edinburgh, Leeds, Liverpool and Manchester (plus a number overseas).

Harvey Nicks is often compared with Harrods (just a stone's throw away), but while Harrods offers huge variety across a massive range of products, HN concentrates on designer clothes, homeware and food, as well as the obligatory beauty department. The store is best known for its fashionable clothes and accessories – it stocks many of the world's most prestigious labels – and attracts a younger clientele than Harrods, which tends to be more upmarket. The fifth-floor food market boasts over 600 exclusive products in Harvey Nicks' smart black and silver livery, along with some luxurious foodie treats and accessories, from gin and tonic popcorn to a champagne sabre.

The store's celebrated restaurant, bar and café have become destinations in their own right and are popular meeting places for savvy shoppers.

Harvey Nichols, 109-125 Knightsbridge, SW1X 7RJ (020-7235 5000; www.harveynichols.com/store/knightsbridge; Knightsbridge tube; Mon-Sat 10am-8pm, Sun noon-6pm).

Hatchards

Hatchards is London's oldest bookshop and the second-oldest in the UK (after the Cambridge University bookshop). It was founded by John Hatchard in 1797 on Piccadilly, from where it still trades today (there's a newer edition at St Pancras station). Customers have included most of Britain's greatest political, royal, social and literary figures – from Queen Charlotte (it boasts three Royal Warrants) to Disraeli, Gladstone to Wellington, Kipling to Lord Byron.

Hatchards is a heady mix of old-world character and personal service, and a favourite with both writers and readers. As such, it has a stellar reputation for attracting famous authors for signings/ readings, from JK Rowling to David Attenborough, Sebastian Faulks to Michael Palin.

Hatchards, 187 Piccadilly, W1J 9LE (020-7439 9921; www.hatchards.co.uk; Piccadilly Circus tube; Mon-Sat 9.30am-8pm, Sun noon-6pm).

House of Hackney

Established in 2010 by Javvy M Royle and Frieda Gormley, House of Hackney was first and foremost a label, although its flagship store in Shoreditch has become a destination for fans of great design. Its aim was 'to take the beige out of interiors', with an emphasis on quality, design and English heritage. The award-winning store stocks all the brand's products, from eiderdowns and furniture to lampshades and wallpaper.

There are many echoes of William Morris around the store; the owners are huge fans of the great textile designer, and were approached in 2015 by the William Morris Gallery to re-imagine Morris for a new generation. The result is a perfect blend of tradition and modernity.

House of Hackney, 131 Shoreditch High St, E1 6JE (020-7613 5559; www.houseofhackney.com; Shoreditch High St rail/Liverpool St tube; Mon-Sat 10am-7pm, Sun 11am-5pm).

John Lewis

Britain's most beloved department store, John Lewis frequently tops surveys of the most popular UK retailers and scores highly on its quality own-brand products and excellent customer service. It offers solid good value (its motto is 'never knowingly undersold'), an unconditional returns policy, and a general feeling of good taste rather than showy fashion. The launch of its Christmas TV advert has become an annual event.

Founded by John Spedan Lewis in 1864, the store has grown from a humble drapery shop to a mighty chain of some 46 stores. One of the most unusual aspects of the John Lewis Partnership – which also owns Peter Jones (see page 241) and the Waitrose supermarket chain – is that it's a limited public company that's held in trust on behalf of its over 90,000 employees or 'partners', all of whom receive an annual share of the profits.

The Oxford Street branch is its undoubted flagship, boating some 20 departments over seven floors, including fashion, beauty, fabrics, homeware, kitchen, electrical goods, toiletries, toys and technology products, along with a splendid Waitrose food hall on the lower ground floor. There's also a coffee shop and a restaurant, plus various fast food outlets.

John Lewis, 300 Oxford St, W1C 1DX (020-7629 7711; www.johnlewis.com/our-shops/oxford-street; Oxford Circus tube; Mon-Wed, Fri-Sat 9.30am-8pm, Thu 9.30am-9pm, Sun noon-6pm).

Liberty

Synonymous with luxury and outstanding design since its launch in 1875, Liberty is one of London's must-visit stores. Arthur Lasenby Liberty's intuitive vision and pioneering spirit led him to travel the world

seeking individual pieces to inspire and excite his discerning clientele. Thus Liberty isn't just a name above the door, but Arthur Liberty's legacy, which stands for integrity, value, quality and, above all, beautiful design – not least the timber-framed, mock-Tudor store built in 1924. (The Liberty staircases are designed in such an odd way that customers often get lost, which led to the publication – in the '70s – of a free booklet entitled 'How Not to Get Lost in Liberty's'!)

Liberty has a long history of artistic and inspiring collaborative projects, from William Morris and Gabriel Dante Rossetti

in the 19th century to Yves Saint Laurent, Mary Quant and Dame Vivienne Westwood in the 20th century. Recent collaborations include renowned brands such as Nike, Kate Moss for Topshop, Hermes and Manolo Blahnik, to name but a few. Nowadays Liberty sells fashions, cosmetics, haberdashery, fabrics, accessories and gifts, in addition to its unique homeware and furniture. When you've soaked up the atmosphere, take a break in the excellent café/restaurant on the second floor.

Unapologetically eccentric and truly innovative, Liberty is a London icon.

Liberty, Regent St, W1B 5AH (020-7734 1234; www.libertylondon.com; Oxford Circus/ Piccadilly Circus tube; Mon-Sat 10am-8pm, Sun noon-6pm).

Lots Road Auctions

Recently made famous nationally by Channel 4's fly-on-the-wall documentary *The Auction House*, Lots Road Auctions in Chelsea was established in 1979 by Roger Ross. It provides an ever-changing eclectic assortment of both contemporary and antique items, ranging from Persian rugs to Matisse etchings, Titchmarsh & Goodwin hand-crafted furniture to Art Deco gems.

In addition to the weekly Sunday auctions – held at noon (modern items) and 3pm (antiques and decorative) – there are regular specialist sales including fine antiques, continental furniture, lighting and mirrors, silver, carpets, tribal and Asian art and artefacts, and Russian art.

Lots Road Auctions, 71-73 Lots Rd, SW10 0RN (020-7376 6800; www.lotsroad.com; Fulham Broadway tube/Imperial Wharf rail; Mon-Tue, Thu, Sun 9am-6pm, Wed 9am-8pm, Fri 9am-5pm, Sat 10am-5pm, check website for viewing and valuation times).

Marcus Watches

The origins of Marcus Watches date back to 1932, when Alexander Margulies (a Polish immigrant) set up business as a clock and watch salesman. He established Time Products, which today owns the Marcus and Hublot fine watch stores on Bond Street as well as Sekonda, the UK's best-selling watch brand.

His son Marcus joined the company in 1963 and has established Marcus Watches as one of the principal 'haute horology' retailers in the world, specialising in complications and tourbillons (the most sophisticated precision timepieces). The New Bond Street boutique is a prime destination for watch lovers, with many rare and unique masterpieces including one of the world's largest collections by renowned Swiss watchmaker Audemars Piguet.

Marcus Watches, 170 New Bond St, W1S 4RB (020-7290 6500; www.marcuswatches.com; Green Pk tube; Mon-Sat 10.30am-5.30pm, closed Sun).

Matches Fashion

Tom and Ruth Chapman opened their first Matches boutique in Wimbledon Village in 1987 and were the first retailers in the UK to stock Prada. Now with five London stores (two in Notting Hill, plus Marylebone, Richmond and Wimbledon) and a massive online business, Matches is one of London's most successful luxury fashion boutiques.

Its Notting Hill store showcases the best of over 400 established and emerging menswear and womenswear designers, from Saint Laurent, Balenciaga, Burberry Prorsum, Christian Louboutin, Chloé and Isabel Marant, to Alexander McQueen, Gucci, Dolce & Gabbana, Diane von Furstenberg, Lanvin, Stella McCartney and Max Mara. Matches also dispenses free fashion advice through its online service, MyStylist.

Matches Fashion, 60-64 Ledbury Rd, W11 2AJ (020-7221 0255; www.matchesfashion.com; Notting Hill Gate tube; Mon-Wed 10am-6pm, Thu-Sat 10am-7pm, Sun noon-6pm).

Melrose & Morgan

Melrose & Morgan in chic Primrose Hill calls itself a 'grocery shop', although it certainly isn't your average corner shop. This grocer-cum-kitchen supplies artisan products and ingredients, as well as freshly prepared meals, for those who care about the quality of their food and its preparation and can afford to pay for the very best. Some two-thirds of M&M's food is made in-house in small batches and what they don't make themselves is carefully sourced from local artisans and independent retailers.

The Primrose Hill shop (their first outlet – there's another in Hampstead) opened in 2004 and has a café where you can enjoy breakfast, lunch or tea, or pick up something for supper.

Melrose & Morgan, 42 Gloucester Ave, NW1 8JD (020-7722 0011; www.melroseandmorgan.com; Chalk Farm tube; Mon-Fri 8am-7pm, Sat 8am-6pm, Sun 9am-5pm).

Ormond Jayne

Launched in 2001 by self-taught 'nose' Linda Pilkington, Ormonde Jayne is a luxury perfume company selling original perfumes, scented candles and bath oils. All products – which bear exotic names such as Orris Noir (based on the Black Iris flower) and Tiare (featuring Tahiti's national flower) – are created by Linda and packaged by hand in her London workshop.

She opened her sumptuous bijou shop – with antique gold wall coverings and black glass chandeliers – in the Royal Arcade in 2006, and has an enviable celebrity clientele list including Elton John, Will Smith and Bryan Ferry.

Ormonde Jayne, 12 Royal Arcade, 28 Old Bond St, W1S 4SL (020-7499 1100; www.ormondejayne.com; Green Pk tube; Mon-Sat 10am-6pm, closed Sun).

Peter Jones

One of the capital's best-loved department stores, Peter Jones occupies an eye-catching Grade II* listed '30s building overlooking Sloane Square. Like many of London's iconic department stores, PJs began as a one-man draper's shop; founded in 1877 by Welshman Peter Rees Jones, it was expanded over the years until it covered most of the block.

It's now owned by John Lewis, and its stock and décor are no different from any other John Lewis store, with departments encompassing fashion, beauty, home and garden, electricals, gifts, toys and more. But there's an air of exclusivity about PJs (as it's affectionately known), no doubt boosted by its reputation for being the spiritual home of the Sloane Ranger.

Peter Jones, Sloane Sq, SW1W 8EL (020-7730 3434; www.johnlewis.com/our-shops/peter-jones; Sloane Sq tube; Mon-Tue, Thu-Sat 9.30am-7pm, Wed 9.30am-8pm, Sun noon-6pm).

Pitfield London

A combination of homeware, design and lifestyle emporium, cool café and trendy art gallery, Pitfield epitomises the spirit of renewal and ingenuity in hip Hoxton. Occupying a huge double-fronted former office block with an edgy, industrial feel, it's the retail arm of celebrated interior designer Shaun Clarkson and business partner Paul Brewster, who have filled the bright, open-plan space with an eclectic assortment of pieces acquired at home and abroad.

Here you'll discover all manner of stylish furniture and home accessories, including colourful '70s seating, vintage glassware and lighting, exclusive Indian rugs, ultra-modern wallpaper from London designers, decorative objects, unique gifts and much more. The blend of old and new, budget-friendly and budget-busting – such as the inexpensive vintage coffee pots lined up alongside Reiko Kaneko's contemporary gold-accented teapots – gives the shop its distinctive character.

The café is an extension of the Pitfield lifestyle and a great place to work,

relax and socialise, while tucking into freshly ground coffee with moreish meringues and brownies, delicious salads and flatbreads. The exhibition space has played host to an array of new and established artists such as Jade Jagger, Louise West, Claire Brewster and James Brown, to name just a few.

Pitfield London, 31-35 Pitfield St, N1 6HB (020-7490 6852; http://pitfieldlondon.com; Old St tube/rail; daily 10am-7pm, see website for café opening hours).

Selfridges

The man who's said to have coined the phrase 'the customer is always right', American entrepreneur Harry Gordon Selfridge was a pioneer of department store retailing and opened his iconic flagship store on Oxford Street in 1909. The second-largest store in the UK after Harrods (see page 234), Selfridges offers one of the most exciting and fashionable shopping experiences in London. Whatever you're after – clothes, bags, shoes, cosmetics, soft furnishings, books, kitchenware, artisan food, etc. – you'll find it in Selfridges.

With its concession boutiques, store-wide themed events and collections from the hottest new brands, it's the first port-of-call for stylish one-stop shopping. If it's luxury you're after, visit the 19,000ft^2 Wonder Room on the ground floor.

Selfridges, 400 Oxford St, W1A 1AB (0800-123 400; www.selfridges.com/london; Bond St tube; Mon-Sat 9am-10pm, Sun noon-6pm).

The Shop at Bluebird

One of London's most acclaimed concept stores, the vast 10,000ft^2 Shop at Bluebird offers a wealth of high-end designers alongside niche labels and emerging fashion talent, interspersed with *objets*, ephemera, books, music and cult beauty brands. Curated by John and Belle Robinson – the creative force behind Jigsaw – Bluebird's team strives to create

an eclectic experience that's both laid back and luxurious, where you can browse and buy the perfect outfit with the help of the store's personal shoppers; there's also a great beauty bar.

It's a stimulating and inspiring taste of vibrant '60s Chelsea, and when you've finished splurging, you can treat yourself to lunch at the Bluebird café next door.

The Shop at Bluebird, 350 King's Rd, SW3 5UU (020-7351 3873; www.theshopatbluebird.com; Sloane Sq tube; Mon-Sat 10am-7pm, Sun noon-6pm).

V&A Shop

The V&A Shop at South Kensington's Victoria & Albert Museum (see page 148) – the world's greatest museum of art and design – is a destination in its own right and a treasure trove of over 6,000 products. The store stocks a broad range of beautiful original designs to suit all ages and pockets, as well as exclusive commissions, one-off vintage pieces and iconic products inspired by exhibits in the V&A's collections and

textiles, toys, ceramics, fashion, design, glass and accessories, which are selected and commissioned from designers and artists throughout the world such as Lulu Guinness, Helen David, Lizzie Montgomery and Walker + Walker.

The shop is a fascinating place to browse or find an unusual present, and there's also an excellent art bookshop. And when you've had your fill of shopping you can take a break in one of the museum's excellent cafés.

V & A Shop, Victoria & Albert Museum, Cromwell Rd, SW7 2RL (020-7942 2696; www.vandashop. com; S Kensington tube; daily 10am-5.30pm, Fri until 9.40pm).

temporary shows. In 2016 these included Engineering the World (cue architectural jewellery), Clangers, Bagpuss & Co (toys and cards inspired by the children's characters) and Undressed (saucy undies and 'washing line' tights). There's a themed mini-shop for major exhibitions.

The wealth of all-year-round merchandise includes jewellery, furniture, books,

Whole Foods Market

P art of the largest organic food chain in the US, the Whole Foods Market has five UK food emporiums (four in London), of which the Kensington outlet, housed in the former Barkers department store, is the largest, extending to some 80,000ft^2.

Everything here is organic and/or locally sourced and free from artificial preservatives, colourings, flavourings, sweeteners and hydrogenated fats. The store offers a vast choice of products, from fruit and vegetables to meat and dairy – including 100 different olive oils, 40 types of sausage and 50 fresh juices – and is one of

the finest organic retailers in London.

The market also offers a wide range of eating options from a number of different food venues, including oven-baked pizza, dim sum, sushi, wok station, Texas BBQ, soup, salads, burritos and tacos, along with vegetarian and vegan options and a juice bar. There's also a wine hub and bar with wines available by the glass.

Much more than just a food retailer, the shop also has a health and beauty department on the lower ground floor devoted to natural skincare and supplements, plus treatment rooms offering facials, skin care analysis, manicures, massages, nutritional advice, holistic treatments, homeopathic remedies and even yoga.

Whole Foods Market, The Barkers Building, 63-97 Kensington High St, W8 5SE (020-7368 4500; www.wholefoodsmarket.com/stores/kensington; High St Kensington tube; Mon-Sat 8am-10pm, Sun noon-6pm).

London Sketchbook

£10.95

ISBN: 978-1-907339-37-0

Jim Watson

A celebration of one of the world's great cities, London Sketchbook is packed with over 200 evocative watercolour illustrations of the author's favourite landmarks and sights. The illustrations are accompanied by historical footnotes, maps, walks, quirky facts and a gazetteer.

Also in this series:

Cornwall Sketchbook (ISBN: 9781907339417, £10.95)
Cotswold Sketchbook (ISBN: 9781907339108, £9.95)
Devon Sketchbook (ISBN: 9781909282704, £10.95)
Lake District Sketchbook (ISBN: 9781907339097, £9.95)
Yorkshire Sketchbook (ISBN: 9781909282773, £10.95)

see www.survivalbooks.net

INDEX

London's Best-Kept Secrets

ISBN: 978-1-909282-74-2, 320 pages, £10.95

David Hampshire

London Best-Kept Secrets brings together our favourite places – the 'greatest hits' – from our London's Secrets series of books. We take you off the beaten tourist path to seek out the more unusual ('hidden') places that often fail to register on the radar of both visitors and residents alike. Nimbly sidestepping the chaos and queues of London's tourist-clogged attractions, we visit its quirkier, lesser-known, but no less fascinating, side. *London Best-Kept Secrets* takes in some of the city's loveliest hidden gardens and parks, absorbing and poignant museums, great art and architecture, beautiful ancient buildings, magnificent Victorian cemeteries, historic pubs, fascinating markets and much more.

London's Hidden Corners, Lanes & Squares

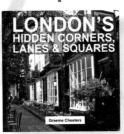

ISBN: 978-1-909282-69-8, 192 pages, £9.95

Graeme Chesters

The inspiration for this book was the advice of writer and lexicographer Dr Samuel Johnson (1709-1784), who was something of an expert on London, to his friend and biographer James Boswell on the occasion of his trip to London in the 18th century, to 'survey its innumerable little lanes and courts'. In the 21st century these are less numerous than in Dr Johnson's time, so we've expanded his brief to include alleys, squares and yards, along with a number of mews, roads, streets and gardens.

A Year in London: Two Things to Do Every Day of the Year

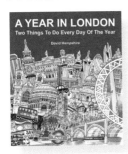

ISBN: 978-1-909282-68-1, 256 pages, £11.95

David Hampshire

London offers a wealth of things to do, from exuberant festivals and exciting sports events to a plethora of fascinating museums and stunning galleries, from luxury and oddball shops to first-class restaurants and historic pubs, beautiful parks and gardens to pulsating nightlife and clubs. Whatever your interests and tastes, you'll find an abundance of things to enjoy – with a copy of this book you'll never be at a loss for something to do in one of the world's greatest cities.

see www.londons-secrets.com

LONDON'S HIDDEN SECRETS

ISBN: 978-1-907339-40-0

£10.95, 320 pages

Graeme Chesters

A guide to London's hidden and lesser-known sights that aren't found in standard guidebooks. Step beyond the chaos, clichés and queues of London's tourist-clogged attractions to its quirkier side.

Discover its loveliest ancient buildings, secret gardens, strangest museums, most atmospheric pubs, cutting-edge art and design, and much more: some 140 destinations in all corners of the city.

LONDON'S HIDDEN SECRETS VOL 2

ISBN: 978-1-907339-79-0

£10.95, 320 pages

Graeme Chesters & David Hampshire

Hot on the heels of London's Hidden Secrets comes another volume of the city's largely undiscovered sights, many of which we were unable to include in the original book. In fact, the more research we did the more treasures we found, until eventually a second volume was inevitable.

Written by two experienced London writers, LHS 2 is for both those who already know the metropolis and newcomers wishing to learn more about its hidden and unusual charms.

LONDON'S SECRET PLACES

ISBN: 978-1-907339-92-9

£10.95, 320 pages

Graeme Chesters & David Hampshire

London is one of the world's leading tourist destinations with a wealth of world-class attractions. These are covered in numerous excellent tourist guides and online, and need no introduction here. Not so well known are London's numerous smaller attractions, most of which are neglected by the throngs who descend upon the tourist-clogged major sights. What London's Secret Places does is seek out the city's lesser-known, but no less worthy, 'hidden' attractions.

LONDON'S SECRET WALKS

ISBN: 978-1-907339-51-6

£11.95, 320 pages

Graeme Chesters

London is a great city for walking – whether for pleasure, exercise or simply to get from A to B. Despite the city's extensive public transport system, walking is often the quickest and most enjoyable way to get around – at least in the centre – and it's also free and healthy!

Many attractions are off the beaten track, away from the major thoroughfares and public transport hubs. This favours walking as the best way to explore them, as does the fact that London is a visually interesting city with a wealth of stimulating sights in every 'nook and cranny'.

see www.londons-secrets.com

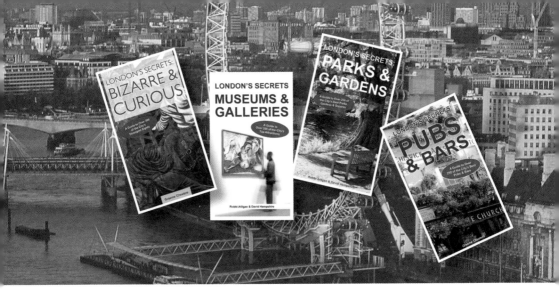

LONDON'S SECRETS:
BIZARRE & CURIOUS
ISBN: 978-1-909282-58-2
£11.95, 320 pages
Graeme Chesters

London is a city with 2,000 years of history, during which it has accumulated a wealth of odd and strange sights. This book seeks out the city's most bizarre and curious attractions and tells the often fascinating story behind them, from the Highgate vampire to the arrest of a dead man, a legal brothel and a former Texas embassy to Roman bikini bottoms and poetic manhole covers, from London's hanging gardens to a restaurant where you dine in the dark. *Bizarre & Curious* is sure to keep you amused and fascinated for hours.

LONDON'S SECRETS:
MUSEUMS & GALLERIES
ISBN: 978-1-907339-96-7
£10.95, 320 pages
Robbi Atilgan & David Hampshire

London is a treasure trove for museum fans and art lovers and one of the world's great art and cultural centres. The art scene is a lot like the city itself – diverse, vast, vibrant and in a constant state of flux – a cornucopia of traditional and cutting-edge, majestic and mundane, world-class and run-of-the-mill, bizarre and brilliant.

So, whether you're an art lover, culture vulture, history buff or just looking for something to entertain the family during the school holidays, you're bound to find inspiration in London.

LONDON'S SECRETS:
PARKS & GARDENS
ISBN: 978-1-907339-95-0
£10.95, 320 pages
Robbi Atilgan & David Hampshire

London is one the world's greenest capital cities, with a wealth of places where you can relax and recharge your batteries. Britain is renowned for its parks and gardens, and nowhere has such beautiful and varied green spaces as London: magnificent royal parks, historic garden cemeteries, majestic ancient forests and woodlands, breathtaking formal country parks, expansive commons, charming small gardens, beautiful garden squares and enchanting 'secret' gardens.

LONDON'S SECRETS:
PUBS & BARS
ISBN: 978-1-907339-93-6
£10.95, 320 pages
Graeme Chesters

British pubs and bars are world famous for their bonhomie, great atmosphere, good food and fine ales. Nowhere is this more so than in London, which has a plethora of watering holes of all shapes and sizes: classic historic boozers and trendy style bars; traditional riverside inns and luxurious cocktail bars; enticing wine bars and brew pubs; mouth-watering gastro pubs and brasseries; welcoming gay bars and raucous music venues. This book highlights over 250 of the best.

see www.londons-secrets.com

London's Secrets: Peaceful Places

ISBN: 978-1-907339-45-5, 256 pages, hardback, £11.95
David Hampshire

London is one of the world's most exciting cities, but it's also one of the noisiest; a bustling, chaotic, frenetic, over-crowded, manic metropolis of over 8 million people, where it can be difficult to find somewhere to grab a little peace and quiet. Nevertheless, if you know where to look London has a wealth of peaceful places: places to relax, chill out, contemplate, meditate, sit, reflect, browse, read, chat, nap, walk, think, study or even work (if you must) – where the city's volume is muted or even switched off completely.

London for Foodies, Gourmets & Gluttons

ISBN: 978-1-909282-76-6, 288 pages, hardback, £11.95
David Hampshire & Graeme Chesters

Much more than simply a directory of cafés, markets, restaurants and food shops, *London for Foodies, Gourmets & Gluttons* features many of the city's best artisan producers and purveyors, plus a wealth of classes where you can learn how to prepare and cook food like the experts, appreciate fine wines and brew coffee like a barista. And when you're too tired to cook or just want to treat yourself, we'll show you great places where you can enjoy everything from tea and cake to a tasty street snack; a pie and a pint to a glass of wine and tapas; and a quick working lunch to a full-blown gastronomic extravaganza.

London's Cafés, Coffee Shops & Tearooms

ISBN: 978-1-909282-80-3, 192 pages, £9.95
David Hampshire

This book is a celebration of London's flourishing independent cafés, coffee shops and tearooms – plus places serving afternoon tea and breakfast/brunch – all of which have enjoyed a renaissance in the last decade and done much to strengthen the city's position as one of the world's leading foodie destinations. With a copy of *London's Cafés, Coffee Shops & Tearooms* you'll never be lost for somewhere to enjoy a great cup of coffee or tea and some delicious food.

see www.londons-secrets.com